A History of British McCalls

by John Stuttard

To the memory of my Mother-in-law,
Elizabeth Daish (nee McCall)
(1919 – 2004)

The text of this book is based on research and information obtained from many sources which are listed in the Bibliography at the end of the book. I have sought to write a compilation of everything I have been able to find about one branch of the British McCalls and then complement this with details of the political, economic, business and social environment in which these McCalls lived. I am grateful to the authors of the books and websites so listed for information about the historical context in which the McCalls carried on business and about individual members of the family over a period of 270 years.

ISBN 978-0993374937

Published by John Stuttard, Shaftesbury

Copyright © John Stuttard

February 2016

Contents

Line of Descendancy from William McCall to Lesley Stuttard (nee Daish)

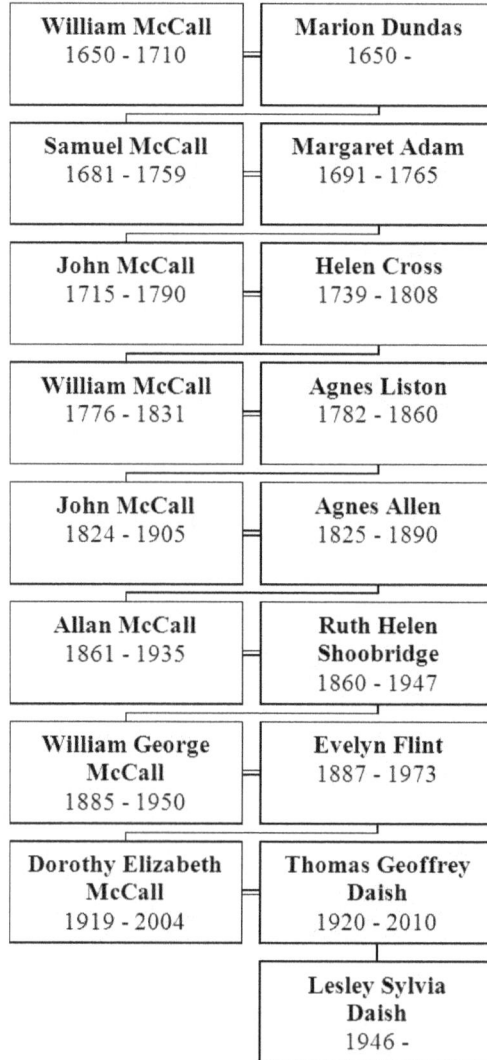

William McCall 1650 - 1710	**Marion Dundas** 1650 -
Samuel McCall 1681 - 1759	**Margaret Adam** 1691 - 1765
John McCall 1715 - 1790	**Helen Cross** 1739 - 1808
William McCall 1776 - 1831	**Agnes Liston** 1782 - 1860
John McCall 1824 - 1905	**Agnes Allen** 1825 - 1890
Allan McCall 1861 - 1935	**Ruth Helen Shoobridge** 1860 - 1947
William George McCall 1885 - 1950	**Evelyn Flint** 1887 - 1973
Dorothy Elizabeth McCall 1919 - 2004	**Thomas Geoffrey Daish** 1920 - 2010

Lesley Sylvia Daish 1946 -

Foreword

Shortly after I married Lesley in 1970, her mother, Elizabeth Daish (nee McCall), lent me two books which had been written and published by her great uncle, Hardy Bertram McCall. They are *Memoirs of My Ancestors – A Collection of Genealogical Memoranda Respecting Several Old Scottish Families*, 1884 and *Some Old Families – A Contribution to the Genealogical History of Scotland*, 1889. Each book contains a chapter on the McCall family, together with Appendices, which relate the history of the McCalls and include family trees from early times in Dumfriesshire until the second half of the 19th century in Great Britain, the American Colonies and South America.

Elizabeth also narrated the recent history of the family business, McCall & Co. This was the last in a succession of McCall businesses, which thrived in different guises and with slightly different names from the early 1700's to the 1970's, a period of 270 years. During this time there were several cycles of endeavour, achievement, success, wealth, a decline in fortunes and financial failure. These cycles were partly as a result of entrepreneurial and opportunistic risk taking – sometimes with fortunate and sometimes with unfortunate consequences. But they also owed much to the political and economic changes of the day, including the 1707 Acts of Union, the American War of Independence, the Napoleonic Wars, Great Britain's naval supremacy post Trafalgar, the Boer War, the First World War, the Great Depression and the UK's Admission to the European Union. These events brought significant changes as well as opportunities and challenges. The cycles were also influenced by changes in technology, including the advent of canning and refrigeration as means of preserving food.

Being an accountant, I was fascinated by the financial rollercoaster that was a feature of Elizabeth and Lesley's McCall family fortunes over a period of 270 years. It was not just a case of rags to riches and back to rags in three generations. Sometimes this happened in one generation and then the cycle kept repeating itself over seven or eight generations. Throughout this fascinating story I was amazed at the family's ability to reinvent itself, in different locations – from Glasgow to America, to Liverpool, to London, to South America and to Tasmania - and in different merchanting activities, from tobacco to general provisions to preserved produce. It is also striking how, in almost every generation, the sons, in their late teens or early twenties, left home to take advantage of opportunities elsewhere and to earn their fortunes. What an entrepreneurial lot they were and, perhaps, they still are.

I imagine that there are many Scottish families whose stories are similar. Travel, exploiting opportunities in foreign lands, enterprise, financial success and failure have all been a feature of the Scots over, at least, the last 300 years. The McCalls seem to be an extreme example, which I was intrigued to research, to follow and to record.

In addition to making interesting reading, I hope that this book will give inspiration to future generations to take advantage of life's chances, as and when they occur, and to take reasonable risks before becoming too settled in their lives.

Sir John Stuttard
February 2016

Line of Descendancy from John McCall or McCaule or McCaull of Dumfriesshire to William McCall, who married Marion Dundas in 1679

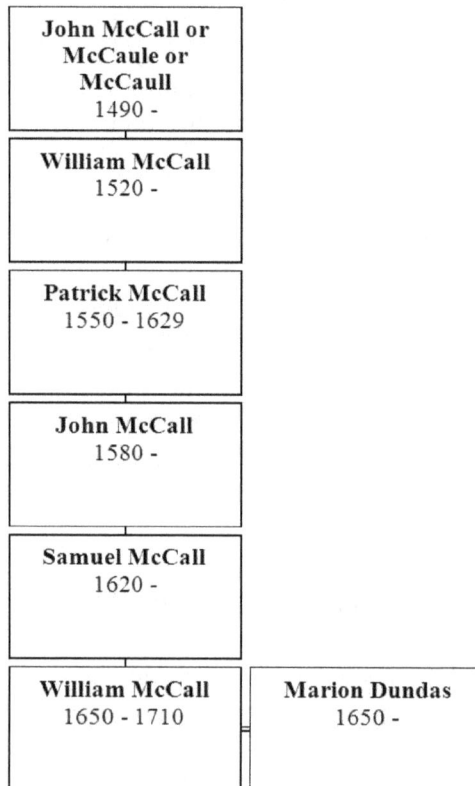

John McCall or McCaule or McCaull 1490 -
William McCall 1520 -
Patrick McCall 1550 - 1629
John McCall 1580 -
Samuel McCall 1620 -

William McCall 1650 - 1710	**Marion Dundas** 1650 -

Origins in the County of Dumfries

It rains a lot in Dumfriesshire.

Each day, its inhabitants have a 50% chance of getting soaked – by a heavy shower or a penetrating misty drizzle. Wet weather gear and thick tweeds are much in evidence.

Indeed, the Scots have many words to describe their damp conditions:
- *Dreich* means wet and dismal
- *Dribble* is drizzle, as well as *mizzle*
- *Smirr* is light rain
- *Dreep* is a steady fall of light rain
- *Plowtery* is showery
- *Greetie* is another word for showery
- *Plype* is a sudden heavy shower
- *Candiegow* is a squall or heavy shower
- *Plump* or *Pishout* is a downpour
- *Sump* is a great fall of rain

A wholesome 900 millimetres, that's 35 inches in old parlance, fall each year on the county's Southern Uplands, making the land green and fertile. While clouds from the Atlantic Ocean drop most of their contents on Ireland, there is still enough left for the Lake District and Dumfries on the Solway Firth, an inlet at the north eastern end of the Irish Sea.

But the wet weather systems also bring a maritime climate to Dumfriesshire, such that there are cool summers and mild winters. The northern part of the county is hilly and bare; the valleys (the dales) to the south are soft and beautiful. There is fine pasture and good arable land, and the rivers are blessed with salmon and trout.

It was to this benign environment, at Ellisland Farm, just north of Dumfries by the River Nith, that Robert Burns came to live in 1788 and where he wrote some of his best poetry. In between farming his 170 acres, he composed memorable poems, including: *A Red, Red Rose, My Love She's But a Lassie Yet, The Whistle, Auld Lang Syne* and this one:

The Banks Of Nith

The Thames flows proudly to the sea,
Where royal cities stately stand;
But sweeter flows the Nith to me,
Where Comyns ance had high command.
When shall I see that honour'd land,
That winding stream I love so dear!
Must wayward Fortune's adverse hand
For ever, ever keep me here!

How lovely, Nith, thy fruitful vales,
Where bounding hawthorns gaily bloom;
And sweetly spread thy sloping dales,
Where lambkins wanton through the broom.
Tho' wandering now must be my doom,
Far from thy bonie banks and braes,
May there my latest hours consume,
Amang the friends of early days!

Children of Willam McCall & Marion Dundas

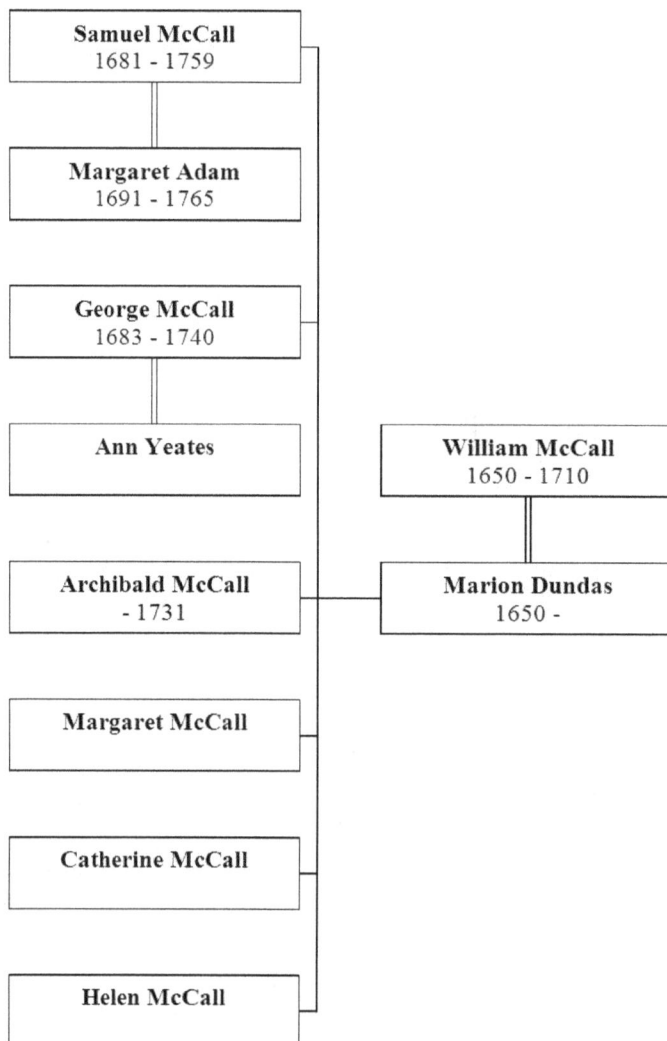

```
┌─────────────────────┐
│   Samuel McCall      │
│    1681 - 1759       │
└─────────────────────┘
┌─────────────────────┐
│   Margaret Adam      │
│    1691 - 1765       │
└─────────────────────┘

┌─────────────────────┐
│   George McCall      │
│    1683 - 1740       │
└─────────────────────┘
┌─────────────────────┐
│    Ann Yeates        │
└─────────────────────┘                  ┌─────────────────────┐
                                          │   William McCall     │
                                          │    1650 - 1710       │
                                          └─────────────────────┘
┌─────────────────────┐                  ┌─────────────────────┐
│  Archibald McCall    │                  │   Marion Dundas      │
│      - 1731          │                  │    1650 -            │
└─────────────────────┘                  └─────────────────────┘

┌─────────────────────┐
│  Margaret McCall     │
└─────────────────────┘

┌─────────────────────┐
│  Catherine McCall    │
└─────────────────────┘

┌─────────────────────┐
│   Helen McCall       │
└─────────────────────┘
```

Twenty or so miles further up the Nith valley, at Penpont and in the nearby village of Kirkconnel, north of Sanquhar, the McCall family had farmed for centuries. Successive generations owned and tenanted small estates. A number of charters dating from the 16th and 17th centuries record land purchases and sales by Maccawls, MacCawles, McCaulls and, finally, McCalls, on which subsequent spelling of the surname has standardised.

Life cannot have been that easy without modern agricultural methods and machinery. The work would have been back breaking – digging dykes by hand; manual ploughing albeit assisted by the family's horse; reaping and collecting hay with scythes and pitchforks; and hay was required in huge quantities to keep cattle and sheep alive through the long winters. Sileage, disease-resistant strains of crops and tractors had not yet been invented. Warm fires and cooking stoves necessitated peat to be dug; water came from the well; and there was a stiff walk to the market at Sanquhar, some 4 miles away, to carry one's produce or to herd the flock for sale. Without modern medicine and health care, children as well as animals died young.

Then, at the turn of the 18th century, the fortunes of a branch of the McCall family changed.

William McCall, who was born in 1650, had taken over his father's farm at Kelloside, in the parish of Kirkconnel, situated, as its name implies, by the side of the Kelloch or Kello-water, a tributary of the River Nith. At the age of 29, in 1679, William made what is called a *good marriage* – to Marion Dundas, daughter of Sir James Dundas, 1st Lord of Arniston.

Marion was the fifth child of Sir James and Marion, nee Boyd, daughter of Robert, Lord Boyd. The noble Scottish families of Dundas and Boyd are both of illustrious descent, whose ancestors include many early kings of Scotland: Donald, Malcolm, Kenneth, Duncan and Robert the Bruce; as well as Llewellyn the Great Prince of North Wales; many Saxon kings of England: Alfred the Great and Ethelred the Unready; and Charlemagne the Holy Roman Emperor.

This was indeed a good catch for William, brought about, one surmises, by the death of Marion's father, also in 1679, and by Marion's need to find a husband and a home away from Arniston which her elder brother, Robert, the 2nd Lord Arniston, had just inherited.

One imagines that Marion brought contacts as well as some small wealth to the McCall household. But, more interestingly, because of her background and upbringing, she must also have opened the eyes of her sons to the possibility of a career outside farming. There were many opportunities being created by England's growing global trade. These were much enhanced by the move towards political and economic union, culminating in Scotland's enhanced trading rights and commercial position after the *Acts of Union* came into force between England and Scotland in 1707.

Their two elder sons, Samuel (1681-1759) and George (1683-1740) were to enjoy hugely successful careers in Glasgow, Maryland & Virginia, and, in Philadelphia, respectively. They were given the chance and they took it.

The third son, Archibald, was less ambitious and succeeded his father as a tenant at Kelloside after William McCall died in 1710.

The World is your Oyster

William's eldest son, Samuel, travelled from Kirkconnell to Glasgow in the last decade of the 17th century. By that time, the city was already experiencing growth and was beginning to take off. Glasgow was becoming a major trading port, on the back of sugar imports and refining and with tobacco coming from North America.

A McCall family story goes that Samuel was sent, when a boy, to the care of a friend of his father's (or was it, actually, his mother's?) in Glasgow, where he was apprenticed and became an extremely successful merchant. His journey from Kirkconnell did not start well. Apparently, he bade farewell to his parents and set out with his sister, crossing the river Nith to the main road, not far from the farm, to wait for the coach and horses to take him to the big city. The carrier was longer coming than expected and the youngsters either fell asleep or wandered away from the road, during which time the waggon passed. So Samuel had to return home, with his tail between his legs, to wait for another opportunity. Father gave him a right roasting, which Samuel so resented that this caused a breach in correspondence between the young man and his family for quite some time.

But the timing of Samuel's move to Glasgow was propitious. The city was about to witness an economic and commercial explosion.

In 1651, the English Parliament passed its Navigation Acts. These acts were mainly aimed at curbing Dutch maritime activity and tightened control over trade between England, its colonies, and the rest of the world. They provided that only English ships could be used for:

- Importing goods from Asia and Africa
- Importing goods from non-English America
- Exports from England's American North Colonies
- Importing goods from Europe
- Any cod, herring, and other fish, fish oil, or whale products

However, these acts also adversely impacted upon Scottish vessels trading from Scottish ports. They limited the ability of Scots to trade with England and its colonies. To do so was against the law, which was often broken by Scottish merchants.

The 1707 Acts of Union resulted in the opening up of opportunities for Scottish merchants who increased in number in Glasgow and abroad, particularly in North America. These opportunities stemmed from some very specific provisions regarding trade, duties and excise contained in the *Union with Scotland Act* passed by the Parliament of England in 1706.

Article IIII provided:
> ### *Trade and Navigation and other Rights.*
> *That all the Subjects of the United Kingdom of Great Britain shall from and after the Union have full freedom and Intercourse of Trade and Navigation to and from any port or place within the said United Kingdom and the Dominions and Plantations thereunto belonging. And that there be a Communication of all other Rights Privileges and Advantages which do or may belong to the Subjects of either Kingdom except where it is otherwise expressly agreed in these Articles.*

Article VI provided:

__Regulations of Trade, Duties, &c.__
That all parts of the United Kingdom for ever from and after the Union shall have the same Allowances Encouragements and Drawbacks and be under the same prohibitions restrictions and regulations of Trade and liable to the same Customs and Duties on Import and Export. And that the Allowances Encouragements and Drawbacks prohibitions restrictions and regulations of Trade and the Customs and Duties on Import and Export settled in England when the Union commences shall from and after the Union take place throughout the whole United Kingdom.

Article VII provided:

__Excise.__
That all parts of the United Kingdom be for ever from and after the Union liable to the same Excise upon all exciseable Liquors.

This Act was followed by *The Union with England Act*, which was passed by the Parliament of Scotland in 1707, ratifying and approving the Union of the two kingdoms of England and Scotland and so creating the United Kingdom of Great Britain.

Prior to the *Acts of Union*, Scottish merchants did not have the same trading and commercial rights as their English counterparts. As a result, before 1707, Whitehaven rather than Glasgow was the largest sea port north of Liverpool on the north western coast of the British mainland, mainly exporting coal from the Lowther estates. This attractive town on the Cumbrian coast continued to thrive in the 18th century on the back of the tobacco trade with North America, with a fleet of some 440 ships and a population of over 9,000 by 1800.

During the first half of the 18th century, Glasgow gradually overtook Whitehaven as a trading port, as a result of the enhanced trading rights and through the enterprise of Glasgow merchants such as Samuel McCall and his offspring. Glasgow became the main port in Europe for importing tobacco from the North American Colonies of Virginia and Maryland. The population of the city grew from around 12,000 in 1700 to 84,000 by 1800.

Like Dick Whittington in London three centuries before him, Samuel McCall was apprenticed in Glasgow, learnt fast and worked hard. In 1707 he married wisely. His wife was Isobel Blackburn, the daughter of a respected Glasgow merchant, by whom he had five children but just one surviving child, Samuel junior, who was born in 1710 and who emigrated to Philadelphia in 1733. Isobel died in 1713.

In the following year, Samuel McCall, senior, married again, to Margaret Adam, daughter of another respected Glasgow merchant, the late John Adam, an elder statesman of the city's Merchant's House, to whom John left the sum of £100 Scots for the Poor on his death in 1704. The Adams were a longstanding family of repute in Glasgow.

By his marriage to Margaret Adam, Samuel McCall, senior, had eight children, the eldest of which, John McCall (1715-1790), became a tobacco merchant like his father. The story of Samuel senior and his son John, as two of Glasgow's *Tobacco Lords* and contributors to Glasgow's business, economic and social success, is told in a later chapter of this book.

8

Meanwhile, William and Marion's second son, George (1683-1740), still in his late teens, left Kirkconnell in 1701 and, after crossing the Atlantic, settled in the neighbourhood of Philadelphia which William Penn had founded in 1682. He married, in 1716, Ann Yeates, the daughter of Judge Jasper Yeates, a member of the city's Council, and of Catherine Sandilands, a granddaughter of the legendary Jöran Kyn, the Swedish founder of Upland, now named Chester, Pennsylvania. George became a prosperous merchant as well as a public servant, being elected a Common Councilman of Philadelphia in October 1722. With his wealth, in 1735 he acquired from the Honourable John Penn, for the sum of 2,000 guineas, on the east side of the Schusekill River, a tract of land amounting to 14,000 acres, which he named *Douglas Manor*. George's second son, Samuel, became Governor of the province and his fifth son, Archibald, became the wealthiest merchant in Philadelphia after engaging in the East India trade. George died in 1740. A local judge ordered his property to be surveyed in order to divide it equally amongst his children. The results of this survey are contained in a tenant map in *The Orphan's Court Docket Book, Volume 3 for Philadelphia County, Pennsylvania in respect of George McCall's Estate*.

As noted earlier, George's nephew, Samuel junior (1710-1761), the only surviving son of his elder brother, Samuel senior, by his first marriage to Isobel Blackburn, also emigrated to Philadelphia, in 1733, to become a merchant. A bond was executed by his father in the sum of £150 as part of the provision made for his emigration, dated 30 November 1732, which was discharged by Samuel junior in 1738. From Philadelphia, according to family tradition, Samuel junior went to China to trade and, on the return voyage, was shipwrecked, but was saved by grabbing hold of and then sitting on top of a hen coop which was floating in the water amongst the other wreckage. Young Samuel went on to marry his first cousin, Anne McCall, George's second daughter, in 1737. With help from his uncle in Philadelphia, he became similarly successful and was appointed Mayor of the city and Commissioner of the Peace in 1741. The younger Samuel also took an active part in the defence of the city against anticipated attacks by France and Spain and he acted as one the managers of the Lottery in 1747 to raise money for the construction of fortifications along the river. He was also a founder trustee of the Philadelphia Library. He died in 1761, leaving six daughters.

Two of Samuel senior's sons, James (1726-1803) and Archibald (1734-1814), by his second marriage to Margaret Adam, were also active in America in the 1750's, residing for a time in Essex County, Virginia, where they bought land. James returned to Glasgow in 1757 while Archibald remained and became a successful merchant initially assisting Samuel McCall & Co and then working on his own account. The American Declaration of Independence created problems for Archibald and for his eldest brother, John, who lived in Glasgow and who was a staunch loyalist. After a struggle, Archibald recovered his land, as a later chapter will reveal. However, John lost his all lands in Virginia and Maryland.

George McCall started the US branch of the McCall extended family, which sired many successful McCalls in America over the next 250 to 300 years. One of these was George Archibald McCall (1802-1868) who was the original commander (Brigadier General) of the Pennsylvania Reserve Corps during the Civil War. He also served in the Mexican-American War and in various Indian wars in America.

The Historical Society of Pennsylvania has a collection of McCall family papers covering the period 1764 to 1891, including business and family correspondence, shipping records, clippings, and three business ledgers. The Virginia Historical Society has correspondence between Archibald McCall and his cousin, also a George McCall, between 1777 and 1783, which letters have survived as a result of a legal action in America between the two McCalls, also described in a later chapter.

Back in Scotland, in the graveyard of Sanquhar's St Bride's church, there is a stone erected in 1814 to replace a former one, which was broken, recording the geographical reach of the McCalls in the 18th century. It reads as follows:

In memory of
Samuel McCall in Kellosyde
a Cadet of the family of the
McCalls of Gussockland

Also of his son
William McCall in Kellosyde
born circa 1650 Died 1710

Also of the third son of William,
Archibald McCall in Kellosyde
born circa 1685 Died 1731
Interred here

Also of the eldest son of William,
Samuel McCall J.P.
of Lorimer House, Glasgow and Estates
in the Colonies of Virginia and Maryland
Born at Kellosyde 1st April 1681
Died at Glasgow 1st March 1759
interred in the burying ground
Of Glasgow Cathedral

Also of the second son of William,
George McCall
of Douglas Manor, Montgomery County
in the Colony of Pennsylvania
Born at Kellosyde circa 1683
Died at Philadelphia 13 Oct. 1740
interred in the burying ground
of Christ Church, Philadelphia

It is clear that the McCalls were an enterprising family who looked for opportunities and took their chances in pursuing them in an era when there were significant risks in transatlantic travel, business and politics.

The Tobacco Trade

Tobacco grows wild in much of North and South America. Until Christopher Columbus landed in the West Indies in 1492, Europeans had never seen the plant. Columbus was given dried tobacco leaves as a gift from American Indians, who smoked it, chewed it, "snuffed" it and even made a drink out of it, *chichi*, which was made more palatable by the addition of sugar from cane. The Indians believed that, when they took tobacco, they were visited by the spirits and that the sun god would reveal his secrets.

The leaves of the plant contain *nicotine*, which is a poison, and other drugs which are *sedative,* and therefore soothing, and *narcotic,* which depresses the senses and can act as a pain killer. European sailors and settlers to North American picked up the habit of smoking tobacco quite quickly and leaves were brought back to Europe by the Spanish in the mid-16th century. A Spaniard, Nicolás Monardes, wrote a report on tobacco, in which he claimed that it would remedy 36 health problems. He recommended its use for the relief of *"toothache, falling fingernails, worms, halitosis, lockjaw and even cancer"*.

Sir Walter Raleigh famously brought tobacco to the English Court in 1586 and grew tobacco plants on his estate at Sherborne Castle in Dorset. There is an apocryphal story that, while sitting on a stone seat at his country retreat, Sir Walter was smoking his pipe when a servant approached with a jug of ale. Thinking his master was on fire, he threw the ale all over him.

And, of course, there is the amusing mythical telephone conversation, related by American Comedian Bob Newhart, between Sir Walter Raleigh and the Chief Executive of the *West Indies Company* in England when Raleigh tries to explain his recent shipment of tobacco, including the following monologue by the incredulous Chief Executive:

> *Tob-acco... er, what's tob-acco, Walt?*
> *It's a kind of leaf, huh?*
> *And you bought eighty tonnes of it?!!*
> *Let me get this straight, Walt, you've bought eighty tonnes of leaves? This may come as a kind of a surprise to you Walt but come fall in England, we're kinda upto our...*
> *It isn't that kind of leaf, huh?*
> *Oh, what kind is it then... some special kind of food?*
> *Not exactly?*
> *Oh, it has a lot of different uses, like, what are some of the uses, Walt?*
> *Are you saying 'snuff', Walt?*
> *What's snuff?*
> *You take a pinch of tobacco... and you shove it up your nose. ha! ha! and it makes you sneeze? ha! ha! ha!*

The English settlers in Virginia quickly adapted to the Indian practice of growing and smoking tobacco. Despite efforts to stamp it out by King James I after he came to the throne in 1603, many thought that tobacco was good for them. Indeed it was widely believed that the medicinal qualities were such that most ailments could be cured by taking tobacco. The leaf produced in Virginia was considered to be of the highest quality and was exported to England from 1613 onwards. Its popularity grew and new immigrants to the American Colonies had to be dissuaded from growing tobacco before they planted corn.

Young people in England and Scotland were encouraged to emigrate to North America as Indentured Servants to work for four to five years on the estates after which they were granted freedom and given fifty acres of land. They sowed corn and other crops but quickly moved on to tobacco which could be grown easily from just a handful of seeds. Even though the supply of tobacco increased and, as a result, prices fell, it was still possible to make a good living from growing tobacco in Virginia and Maryland.

After Charles II came to the throne in 1660, he introduced a law banning the Virginia farmers from selling their crops to any country other than England. With the increased supply of tobacco to England, prices fell further and the English merchants, having taken possession of their crops, then sold them on to buyers on the European continent to make ends meet. Thus began the entrepôt trade and the relationships which ultimately led to Glasgow being a major importer of tobacco from North America and then supplying an astonishing one-third of all Europe's demand for this commodity.

Charles II was also a keen sniffer of snuff, a habit he brought with him when he returned from exile in the Netherlands. This encouraged English Society to follow suit. Tobacco sales increased dramatically towards the end of the 17th century and still further over the next 100 years.

Statistics of imports of tobacco from North America to the UK are available, albeit they have been questioned, but the following figures (from the Historical Statistics of the United States, US Department of Commerce, 1975) give some indication of the trend (in pounds weight):

1620	55,000
1635	600,000
1639	1,500,000
1688	18,150,000
1700	38,000,000
1771	100,000,000

In the first half of the 18th century, Glasgow's merchants handled a small proportion of the crop from North America. However by the 1750's this had increased such that Glasgow's share of the trade in tobacco was almost as great as the rest of Britain's ports combined.

The Growth of Glasgow as a Major Port

The English have always been wary of their Northern neighbours.

Some famous military engagements record the enmity:

- 832 – A battle in Lothian at which the forces of Scottish King Angus defeated an Anglo-Saxon army which had chased the raiding Scots out of Northumberland. It was alleged that prior to this battle St Andrew appeared, forecasting a Scottish victory. Then, on the day of the battle, there was a cloud formation of a white saltire, the shape of the cross on which St Andrew was martyred, on a blue sky. The king vowed that if the Scots won, St Andrew would be made the patron saint of Scotland. The Scots did win and a white saltire on a blue background was also adopted as the Scottish flag
- 1296 – The capture of the border town of Berwick by the English, followed by the Battle of Dunbar, an English victory
- 1314 – The Scottish victory over Edward II at Bannockburn
- 1346 – The Battle of Neville's Cross, where the English halted the Scottish invasion of England in Northumberland
- 1513 – The Battle of Flodden, at which the English defeated the army of King James IV in Northumberland. Of interest to our story is that many ancestors of the McCalls, including four through the Dundas line, died in this battle: Sir William Dundas, Colin Oliphant who was Master of Oliphant, William Leslie 3rd Earl of Rothes and Andrew Herries 2nd Lord Herries of Terregles
- 1542 – The Battle of Solway Firth, where the English defeated the army of King James V who was trying to invade England

Writing *Henry V* in 1599, Shakespeare captures the lack of trust in England's northern neighbours. When considering his right to the French throne and making the necessary preparations to wage war prior to the siege of Honfleur and then the Battle of Agincourt in 1415, King Henry V is given these words by the Bard:

> *We must not only arm to invade the French,*
> *But lay down our proportions to defend*
> *Against the Scot, who will make roads upon us*
> *With all advantages*

And still further:

> *For you shall read that my great-grandfather*
> *Never went with his forces into France*
> *But that the Scot on his unfurnished kingdom*
> *Came pouring like the tide into a breach*
> *With ample and brim fullness of his force,*
> *Galling the gleanèd land with hot assays,*
> *Girding with grievous siege castles and towns,*
> *That England, being empty of defense,*
> *Hath shook and trembled at th' ill neighborhood.*

Although James VI of Scotland became James I of England in 1603, suspicion and mistrust between the two countries prevented any closer union for the next century. The Scots feared that they would be swallowed up and become just another region of England. On the other side, the English feared that the Scots would forge alliances with France and might even provide soldiers to fight for England's longstanding foe. Thus the Acts of Union were delayed for 100 years.

The 1603 union of the Scottish and English crowns did however stimulate trade between the two countries. In 1611, a Royal Charter granted Glasgow the status of a burgh which made a minor dent in the controlling power of the local bishops. But it wasn't until 1690 that the town achieved self-governance when the council was given the right to elect its own Provost and the two Baillies. During the first half of the 17th century, Glasgow was still a small port with its overseas trading activities limited mainly to herring and sugar, which were exported to England and, perhaps illegally, to Scotland's old ally, France. As time went on, trade also developed in cotton, textiles and tobacco and the economy grew.

By 1700 when young Samuel McCall had settled in Glasgow, the city was small with a population of just 12,000. The houses and shops were clustered around Glasgow Cathedral and the Glasgow Cross at the eastern end of Trongate, which was so named after the site of the *tron* which was a beam used for weighing goods brought to market. *Tron* is derived from the old French word *trone* for scales. *Gait* is the old Scots word meaning "*the way to*". The eastern edge of the town was the Molendinar Burn which flows in a north-south direction into the River Clyde.

In the previous century, with the city's growing wealth, the inhabitants had erected some important public buildings:
- In 1626, a new Tolbooth was constructed in the heart of the city at Glasgow Cross. Here, in days gone by, anyone bringing goods into the burgh would have paid dues after the goods had been weighed on the *tron*. The building, now demolished, next to the steeple which remains to this day, was used as the Council's Chambers. It also served as a small prison and was next to the site of public hangings. The Tolbooth steeple was, and still is, quite a landmark, some seven stories high, with a crown spire on the top standing at the end of Trongate
- Hutchesons' Hospital was built in the 1640's in Trongate. This was pulled down and replaced in1805 by Hutchesons' Hall, which can be found today in Ingram Street
- The University, which had been founded in 1451, was enlarged in the 17th century with Old College constructed in 1656
- Reflecting the growing mercantile trade, a new Merchants' Hall was completed in 1659, for the long established Merchants' House, of which more later. A very tall steeple was added in 1665 to provide a lookout for ships as well as demonstrating the status and wealth of the Glasgow merchants. This tower still stands today
- New churches were built such as Blackfriars which had been destroyed after being hit by lightning in 1670.

Writing in 1723, John Macky described Glasgow as "the beautifullest (sic) little city I have seen in Britain".

In 1668, land was acquired on the south side of the River Clyde estuary and Port Glasgow was created. Despite attempts by the English, prior to 1707, to restrict overseas trading by the Scots, Glasgow's merchants succeeded in importing large quantities of sugar from the West Indies and tobacco from North America.

The Scots also wished to participate, like their English neighbours, in overseas colonisation. This led to the ill-fated Darien Scheme in Panama into which many Scottish nobles and towns poured their money in the 1690's. The Darien Scheme was the brainchild of William Paterson who also hailed from Dumfriesshire and whose other claim to fame was founding the Bank of England. Paterson had the idea of linking the Atlantic and the Pacific oceans via a colony in the narrow Darien Isthmus separating North and South America. This would short circuit the long and dangerous voyage around Cape Horn. Originally it was conceived as a joint Anglo-Scottish venture but the British Government withdrew its support under pressure from the East India Company who feared the scheme might impact adversely their monopoly of trade in Asia. About half the wealth of Scotland was invested in the scheme and many Scotsmen volunteered to sail to Panama to establish the colony. Out of 1,200 settlers who sailed in the first five ships, 400 died within half a year from tropical diseases and attacks by Spanish soldiers and colonists. There were quarrels among the elected representatives and the colony failed to get established. Eleven further ships set sail before news of the initial disaster reached Glasgow and, in total, more than 2,000 people did not return to their homes in Scotland. Almost half a million pounds was lost in the scheme, leaving many Scottish families bankrupt. The English Government and the East India Company were blamed for the failure. As part of the negotiations which led to the signing of the Acts of Union, funds were provided by the English to help compensate for the losses sustained in the Darien Scheme. Scotland's leaders realised that they needed to be part of a large trading entity. Threats of continuing English sanctions, including taxes on Scottish imports, also made the status quo impossible. However, the Union did not take place without some dissent and riots took place in Glasgow in 1706 and 1707.

In the British Isles as a whole, in the late 17th century, and more so in the 18th century, there was a gradual increase in trade at the northern ports of Liverpool, Whitehaven and Glasgow at the expense of the more southerly ports of Bristol, Barnstable and Bideford. Bristol did, however, maintain a large share of the transatlantic trade and, as related later, it became the major UK tobacco port again in the 19th century, when Glasgow's dominance was shattered.

To begin with, the Glasgow merchants chartered vessels from Liverpool and elsewhere. In 1718 the first ship owned in the Clyde crossed the Atlantic.

There were a number of reasons, in addition to the change in legislation, for Glasgow's rise to importance as a port: the Glaswegian merchants dealt directly with the planters in Virginia, exchanging goods, such as clothing and manufactured items, for tobacco and cotton; they provided finance to the colonial planters; the northern ports were more efficient and had lower labour costs; by sailing to the north of Ireland, ships from these ports were well away from any hostile naval attacks from France, Holland and Spain in the Channel and the mid-Atlantic; and, most compelling, the journey time across the North Atlantic was much shorter, by as much as two weeks, than the southern routes, so reducing the cost of transport and the wear to ships. The lower cost of goods, particularly of tobacco, passing through Glasgow in the 18th century made the port more competitive than London. Thus, the prices charged by the Glaswegian tobacco merchants to their customers on the Continent were also lower and Glasgow's share of the tobacco trade grew.

Glasgow's geographical position on the River Clyde with its sheltered access to the Atlantic made it the natural location for a major port. Its strategic position was further enhanced by being the lowest crossing point over the river until many years later. Glasgow became the obvious hub for Scotland's growing industrialisation, facilitating the import of commodities and the export of finished goods.

By 1775, Scotland imported 46 million lbs of tobacco compared to 56 million lbs imported by all the English ports. More than 4/5^{ths} of the trade was exported to the Continent and, in the case of Glasgow, Europe's biggest tobacco entrepôt, most of this went to France. It has been estimated that, at its peak, Glasgow supplied 1/3rd of all the tobacco consumed on the Continent.

The tobacco trade was also matched in importance by the import, and later the refining, of sugar, which stimulated other trades such as brewing, distilling and baking, and by the import of cotton, which stimulated textile manufacture in the west of Scotland. The Clyde had been dredged. Nearby canals had been dug and road communication had improved. Glasgow had developed into a major European port and the city had entered a golden era.

As the population grew, the city expanded and the centre moved west. Some fine buildings were constructed in the 18th century as a result of the city's wealth and enhanced status. Prominent among these were:
- The stunning neo-classical Trades Hall, with its dome, designed by Robert Adam and built in 1794
- The McLennan Arch constructed in 1796 as the centrepiece of the Adams' Assembly Rooms and now situated at Glasgow Green
- The Assembly Rooms completed in 1797
- Very many houses built by the Carswell Brothers in Albion Street, Cochrane Street, Miller Street and Richmond Street, as well as Candleriggs

And then, in 1829, the magnificent Royal Exchange was completed, with its huge Corinthian columns facing Queen Street

Glasgow had justifiably become Scotland's second city and would grow, in the 19th century, to become the country's industrial powerhouse of shipbuilding. But, in the 18th century, Glasgow was a city of international trade, until the ruminations on the other side of the Atlantic led to the American wars and the Declaration of Independence in 1776 which threatened the city's prosperity and its economic existence.

The Tobacco Lords of Glasgow

Trade does indeed bring prosperity and Glasgow flourished on the back of it in the 18th century. One of the main groups to stimulate this trade was the tobacco merchants, known as *Tobacco Lords, Tobacco Barons* or *Virginia Dons*. In short order, they were to become the main beneficiaries, amassing huge wealth and privilege. It is not known exactly how many merchants were engaged in the tobacco trade, but estimates have put the number at around 150. There was a small group of very successful tobacco merchants and three in particular: William Cunninghame, Alexander Speirs and John Glassford dominated the tobacco trade through their large syndicates. And they dressed to impress, with black silk or velvet coats, silk stockings, scarlet cloaks, tricorn hats over powdered wigs and gold-headed ebony canes in their hands.

These *Tobacco Lords* were looked up to as the Glasgow aristocracy and in his *Enumeration of the Inhabitants of the City of Glasgow (1832)*, the author, James Cleland wrote: "*When any of the most respectable master tradesmen of the city had occasion to speak to a Tobacco Lord, he required to walk on the other side of the street till he was fortunate enough to meet his eye*".

As described in the above chapter on the tobacco trade, Glasgow' imports and exports grew substantially in the second and third quarters of the 18th century. In his book, *Sketches of the History of Glasgow*, published by Robert Stuart & Co in 1844, James Pagan lists the main importers and the amounts of tobacco imported into the city, in pounds weight, in 1774, almost at the end of the "golden era" of the *Tobacco Lords*, as follows:

1. Alexander Speirs & Co.   6,035,000
2. John Glassford & Co.   4,506,000
3. Wm. Cunninghame & Co.   3,881,000
4. Dinwiddie, Crawford & Co.   2,141,000
5. John Hamilton & Co.   1,967,000
6. Oswald, Dennistoun & Co.   1,701,000
7. Henderson, McCaul & Co.   1,587,000
8. Colin Dunlop & Co.   1,455,000
9. Cunninghame, Findlay & Co.   1,290,000
10. Bogle, Somervill & Co.   1,270,000
11. John Ballantine & Co.   1,245,000
12. James Donald & Co.   1,264,000
13. John McCall & Co.   1,233,000
14. Buchanan, Hastie & Co.   1,085,000
15. John Alston & Co.   1,013,000
16. James Ritchie & Co.   903,000

These *Tobacco Lords* were entrepreneurs. They took great financial risks, sometimes borrowing heavily. And they made great fortunes based on sailing fast across the Atlantic and entering into commercial deals in North America. The Glasgow merchants offered easy credit facilities which in turn were translated into lower prices for the tobacco from the farmers in Virginia and Maryland. At his Mount Vernon plantation, future President of the United States, George Washington, saw his indebtedness swell and Thomas Jefferson accused British merchants of unfairly depressing tobacco prices. In 1786, he wrote: "*A powerful engine for this was the giving of good prices and credit to the planter till they got him more immersed in debt than he could pay without selling lands or slaves. They then reduced the prices given for his tobacco so that…they never permitted him to clear off his debt*". While this did not lead directly to the American War of Independence, it was but one of the many grievances that the North American colonists had against their British overloads.

Back in the 17th century, in 1677 a disastrous fire had destroyed much of Glasgow. The fire, which was started by a malicious apprentice who had been scolded by his master, was also judged to be a sign of God's wrath. The result of the subsequent enquiry was the immediate ban on timber as a material for construction and the introduction of stone. This led to some fine buildings being erected over the next century. The *Sugar Lords* and the *Tobacco Lords,* in particular, commissioned grand houses in, what became known as, "*merchant villa style*".

As Adam Smith wrote, "*Merchants are commonly ambitious of becoming country gentlemen, and when they do, they are generally the best of all improvers. The habits, besides, of order, economy, and attention, to which mercantile business naturally forms a merchant, render him much fitter to execute, with profit and success, any project of improvement*".

These houses were mainly built on the western side of the city which was expanding from its historical location in the east near the Molendinar Burn and the Cathedral. They were a very visual demonstration of the wealth that had been acquired by the *Tobacco Lords* over many decades, particularly in the period 1690 to 1770. Some of these buildings are worthy of particular mention.

- *Germiston House* was built in 1690 by Robert and Lawrence Dinwiddie. Robert became Governor of Virginia while Lawrence became Lord Provost of Glasgow. Like the McCalls, the Dinwiddie family hailed from Dumfries and came to Glasgow in the middle of the 17th century. The house was demolished in 1926
- *Shawfield Mansion* was built in 1711 by Daniel Campbell of Shawfield. There were broad steps up to double front doors which led to a three-storied neo-classical house, with a central capital to the facade. The house stood at the corner of Trongate and Glassford Street (named after another *Tobacco Lord,* John Glassford, who lived at *Shawfield Mansion* in the 1760's). The house was demolished in 1792
- *Drumpellier House* in Coatbridge was constructed in several stages, beginning in 1736, by Andrew Buchanan. Like most of the other grand houses, it was demolished – in the case of *Drumpellier* much later, in the 1960's
- *Craighton House* was acquired by merchant John Ritchie in 1746. It was similar in appearance to the *McCall's Black House* (see below), but with the addition of two square wings. On his death it passed to his son, James, who was also a successful merchant as well as a founding member of Glasgow's *Thistle Bank*, as was John McCall (see below), which was established in 1761. The *Thistle Bank* was known as the aristocratic bank because most of its founding shareholders were major landowners and *Tobacco Lords*
- Andrew Buchanan's son, George, built *Virginia Mansion* in 1752 on the west side of the city with gardens around it. Modelled, one imagines on *Shawfield Mansion*, there were broad steps leading up to double front doors, a balustrade running along the top

of the house around the large pitched roof and four chimneys poking out of the middle of the roof. There were six downstairs and six upstairs windows along the front façade. The house was sold in 1770 to Alexander Speirs and was demolished in 1842 – to be replaced by a bank

- George Buchanan also had a country house, named *Mount Vernon*, on the east side of the city as part of the *Windy Edge Estate*, which he acquired in 1756. Sadly he died at the early age of 34 in 1762 and was not able to appreciate his fine houses for long. *Mount Vernon* was demolished in 1932

- *Belvidere House* was built by John McCall in 1760 to the east of the city on a large plot of land bordering the River Clyde. It was a substantial house with two wings, bowed at the front, and with no fewer than 11 windows on the front façade at first floor level. The mansion was demolished in 1887 after it had been acquired some years earlier by the City Council to be replaced by a large hospital on the site

Belvidere.

- *Elderslie House* was built near Renfrew by Alexander Speirs in 1769 after he acquired the King's Inch Estate. The house was a grand mansion and was demolished in 1920

- *The Tobacco Merchant's House* which was built by John Craig in 1775 along Palladian lines has a central door with pediment, flanked by fluted Corinthian pilasters. It is one of very few significant houses from that period still remaining and was restored in 1995 by the Glasgow Building Preservation Trust which now occupies the building together with the Scottish Civic Trust

- *McCall's Black House* was also built by John McCall, in the 1770's, at the corner of Argyle Street and Queen Street. It had a classical front with double stairs leading to the entrance on the first floor and the house possessed no fewer than 40 windows. It was demolished soon after McCall's death to make way for a tenement building

The Black House.

- *Cunninghame Mansion* was built by William Cunninghame in 1778, just as the lucrative tobacco trade was coming to an end, for a staggering £10,000. Thought to be one of the finest houses in Scotland at the time, it subsequently became part of the Royal Bank of Scotland. In 1996, it was renovated at a cost of £6 million and is now the Gallery of Modern Art. Each year, the Gallery now attracts over 400,000 visitors who are probably oblivious to its origins as a palace built on the back of Glasgow's tobacco trade with Virginia and Maryland.

Sadly for Glasgow's heritage, very few of these great houses have survived. Only literature can testify to the wealth and the gracious living that such mansions would have afforded. Some of the *Tobacco Lords* are remembered by streets named after them: Buchanan, Cochrane, Dunlop, Glassford, Ingram, Oswald and Wilson.

The *Tobacco Lords* even arranged for their own church to be built – St Andrew's in the Square, constructed between 1739 and 1756, whose design was inspired by St Martin-in-the-Fields in London's Trafalgar Square.

For many centuries, throughout Europe, participating in a craft or a trade was controlled and restricted by a guild or, in the case of London, a livery company. These organisations would regulate the training of apprentices and the admission of skilled craftsmen or merchants to the guild such that only its members could engage in the regulated activity. They often dictated prices and monitored quality and exercised disciplinary powers.

In Glasgow, the craftsmen and tradesmen were members of the Trades House, headed by the Deacon Convenor. The merchants were members of the Merchants House, headed by the Dean of Guild. The Merchants House had existed in some form or another for centuries and was formally incorporated in 1605. The Trades House and the Merchants House were enormously powerful. No one could trade or engage in a business activity except through membership of the relevant body. And the merchants were particularly powerful in local politics with the Dean of Guild outranking everyone else, including the Lord Provost.

Today's Merchants House building, dating from 1877, is situated on the corner of George Square and West George Street. The prime aim of the Merchants House, as a charity, is to make grants to various educational institutions and to provide bursaries. By virtue of its history and charters, the Merchants House is still very active in local community affairs and elects representatives to many public institutions, including Hutchesons' Hospital, Hutchesons' Educational Trust, The Adam Smith Chair of Political Economy at Glasgow University, The Chamber of Commerce, The Glasgow Educational and Marshall Trust and The University of Strathclyde.

Unlike their English tobacco merchanting counterparts, who simply sold American tobacco on commission, the Glasgow *Tobacco Lords* went one stage further. As mentioned above, they gave the planters easy credit to finance their operations and also to buy expensive and luxurious goods from Great Britain before the tobacco crop had been harvested. By the time of the American War of Independence, the debts due to the Scottish merchants had accumulated to over £1,300,000. And, as further diversification of their activities, some of the wealthier *Tobacco Lords* had established their own banks such as the *Thistle Bank*.

The financing of American tobacco growers was to prove a major problem for many *Tobacco Lords* during the War of Independence as many of the loans were not repaid and the British Government did not fully compensate the Glasgow merchants for their losses.

But, during the mid-18th Century, the *Tobacco Lords* had riches beyond most people's dreams. As Carolyn Marie Peters writes in her PhD thesis *Glasgow's tobacco lords: an examination of wealth creators in the eighteenth century*, "*They [the Tobacco Lords] had their role as businessmen certainly, but more importantly they were also politicians, members of clubs, acquaintances of Adam Smith, purchasers of great estates which they furnished with the finest mahogany and japanned tables, where they ate off of silver plates and drank the finest coffee in coffee-cans made of delft-ware, and where they drank out of silver chalices filled with the best Madeira wine or French brandy, patrons of the arts and of the theatre, and builders of beautiful churches whose extravagance bespoke of their wealth.*"

As Graham describes in *The Social Life of Scotland in the Eighteenth Century*, "*Life in 18th Century Glasgow was a very ordered affair. Social customs were carried out with precision and work and the tavern went hand in hand with normal everyday life. The usual pattern of the working day in Glasgow for the men usually started at 6:00am when, advertised by a gun, the post from Edinburgh arrived carrying with it correspondence and the Edinburgh papers. After that, the men usually proceeded to their work whether it be in a shop, a small factory, or the counting-house. At mid-day life usually continued in the local taverns or coffee houses where gossip and local information was exchanged. From 2:00pm until the late hour of 8:00pm, work was continued to be followed by perhaps a trip to the tavern*".

J.B.Obernetter.

Samuel McCall
(1681 - 1759)

The 18th Century McCalls, Tobacco Lords of Glasgow

Samuel McCall (1681 – 1759)

As described earlier, Samuel McCall came to Glasgow as a boy, studied diligently, worked hard, married well (twice) and enjoyed a successful career as a tobacco merchant.

Samuel became a wealthy and influential citizen and was made a burgess (a freeman) of the city in 1708 at the age of 27. He owned several vessels which traded with the American colonies and purchased extensive land and tobacco farms in Maryland and Virginia, one of which was named McCall's Manor. Records show that in 1735 one of 15 Glasgow-based vessels which sailed to and from Virginia was the *Betty*, owned by Samuel McCall. He traded under the name "Samuel McCall & Co., Virginia Merchant".

In 1721, Samuel acquired a sizeable house and grounds, with stables and a brew house, together known as *Lorimer's House*, which was named after the previous owner, John Lorimer. The house was situated on the south side of the fashionable Gallowgate, the property being bounded on the east by the Molendinar Burn.

In 1722 Samuel was elected a Councillor and in 1723 he was chosen to be one of the two Baillies (magistrates). Then, in 1736, he was nominated Lord Dean of Guild, which he declined to accept as, in his own words, "*he was very unfit to exert on account of his bad state of health*". It seems as though this was an excuse, as the office was an onerous one and might have adversely affected his ability to run his merchanting business and manage his overseas possessions. According to the custom of the day, he was imprisoned in the Tolbooth for a few hours for refusing to accept the office. Following this, a special act of the Trades House was passed on 2 November 1736 to deal with the situation, through a fine, where one chosen as Dean of Guild or Deacon Convenor refused to accept office.

In the troubles of 1745, he was a loyal supporter of the King and his name is appended to a requisition signed by a large number of inhabitants setting out that "*the city of Glasgow is in danger of being attacked by a force which they are in no condition to resist*" and desiring the six Commissioners, "*in case any such force shall approach the city and require to be lodged therein, that you meet with the Leaders of the said force and make the best terms you possibly can for saving the city and its trade and inhabitants*".

Following the practice of many successful merchants, Samuel McCall had arms. The version which he used initially was as follows: "*Azure a pheon argent on a chief of the last two spur-rowels and part of the spur gules*". His crest was "*A griffin's head between wings*". A later version, used by the family from about 1800, but not registered until 1863 by James McCall (1778 – 1866), one of Samuel's grandsons, is as follows: "*Gules two arrows saltire wise between three buckles argent surmounted by a fesse checquy of the second and sable within a bordure engrailed or*". The crest is "*A leg in armour couped at the calf proper and spurrd or*", with the motto "*Dulce periculum*" translated as "*Danger is sweet*". This crest is contained in signet rings worn by Elizabeth Daish (nee McCall) and by my wife, Lesley.

Children of Samuel McCall & Margaret Adam

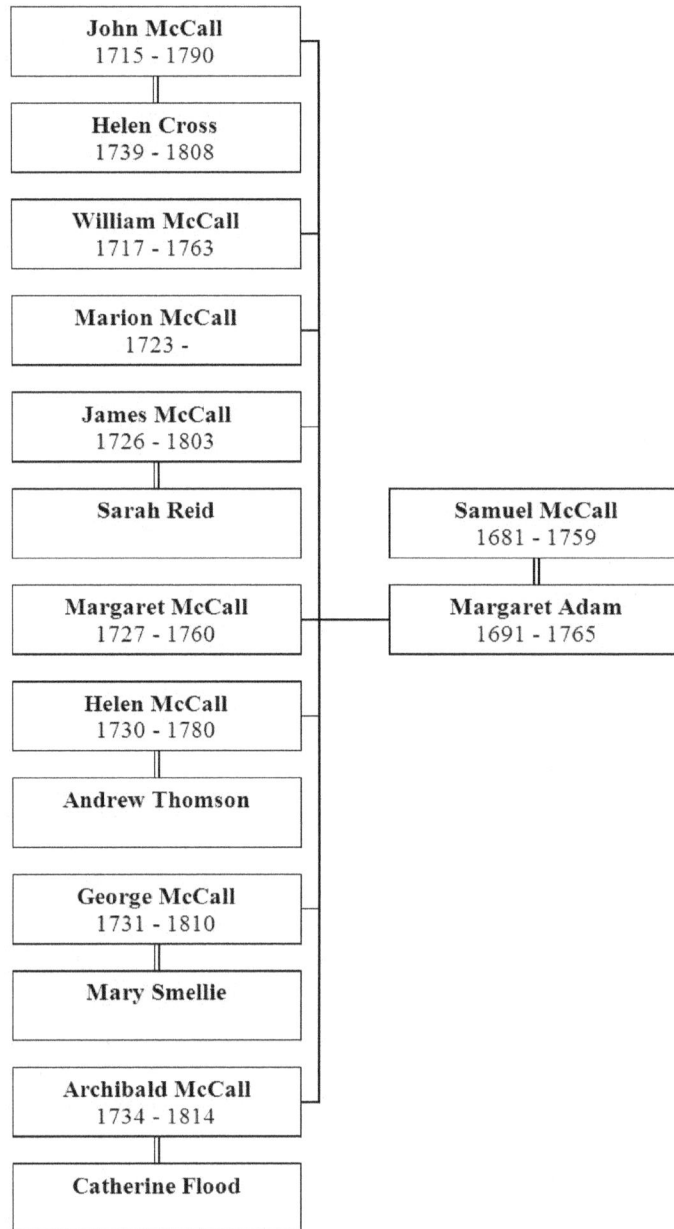

John McCall 1715 - 1790	
Helen Cross 1739 - 1808	
William McCall 1717 - 1763	
Marion McCall 1723 -	
James McCall 1726 - 1803	
Sarah Reid	**Samuel McCall** 1681 - 1759
Margaret McCall 1727 - 1760	**Margaret Adam** 1691 - 1765
Helen McCall 1730 - 1780	
Andrew Thomson	
George McCall 1731 - 1810	
Mary Smellie	
Archibald McCall 1734 - 1814	
Catherine Flood	

24

These later bearings of crest and motto are very similar to those of the Macaulay Clan, to which it is considered that the McCalls owe their origin. Accordingly, the McCalls are, allegedly, entitled to wear the Macaulay tartan, of which there are two varieties:

- Hunting – Dark green with black, red and white stripes
- Dress – Bright red with black, green and white stripes.

By his second wife, Margaret Adam, Samuel McCall had eight children who survived their youth:

- John McCall, born 27 March 1715, Glasgow (see below)
- William McCall, born 4 January 1717, Glasgow. He was a merchant in Glasgow in partnership with his father and afterwards with his brothers John and James. He was made a burgess and guild-brother (both types of freeman) of the city on 11 October 1748. He never married and died in Glasgow in December 1763
- Marion McCall, born 4 June 1723, Glasgow. She married John Anderson who was a merchant in Glasgow
- James McCall, born 31 May 1726, Glasgow. He spent some years in Essex County, Virginia in the 1750's where he bought land for his father. He returned to Scotland in 1757, leaving his younger brother Archibald in charge. On 27 January 1761, he married Sarah Reid, daughter of Thomas Reid, merchant in Saltcoats, Ayrshire, and is the ancestor of the McCalls of Glyntown, County Cork in Ireland, and the McCalls of Daldowie, Lanarkshire. (See Burke's Landed Gentry). He lived in Braehead, Renfrewshire and he died in Glasgow on 20 March 1803
- Margaret McCall, born 5 September 1727, Glasgow. She died on 26 July 1760
- Helen McCall, born 4 January 1730, Glasgow. She married on 13 November 1749 Andrew Thomson of Faskine, merchant and banker in Glasgow and founder of the London banking firm of Thomson, Bonar and Co. She died on 23 September 1780
- George McCall, born 10 April 1731, Glasgow. He was a merchant in Fredericksburg and Spotsylvania County, Virginia; but he afterwards returned to Scotland. He was a Virginia merchant in Glasgow, in partnership with Archibald Smellie, He married Mary, sister of his business partner and daughter of Archibald Smellie of Easterhill, Stirlingshire. He died at his residence on the west side of Queen Street, Glasgow, on 20 February 1810, leaving a large family. He was the grandfather of James McCall of Glasgow and of Colonel George McCall, Master of the Horse at the Court of King Louis Philippe of France
- Archibald McCall, born 28 April 1734, Glasgow. He emigrated to Essex County, Virginia in the 1750's, acting for the McCall family business. During the American War of Independence he returned to Great Britain, but travelled back to America after the troubles ceased in 1783. He married Catherine Flood, a Virginian, the only daughter of Dr Nicholas & Eliza Flood. Archibald died in Richmond, Virginia in 1814, leaving a daughter, Catherine-Flood McCall, who died unmarried.

Samuel died in January 1759 at the age of 77 and was buried in a vault which he had commissioned many years earlier in the burial ground outside the east end of Glasgow Cathedral. An inscribed stone states "*The burying place appointed for Samuel McCall (1681 – 1759), Merchant of Glasgow, and Margaret Adam his spous* (sic) *and their children*". He left his property in various proportions to the eight children who survived him, with a life interest to Margaret, who died in 1765. He also left £15 sterling to the "*Poor of the Merchants House*".

John McCall (1715–1790)

John McCall was Samuel's eldest son by his marriage to Margaret Adam. John entered and then took over his father's business. He also traded under the name "John McCall & Co, Tobacco Importers". He was as successful as his father and perhaps even more so.

In 1748 he was made a burgess, like his father.

In 1757 John put forward a motion to the Merchants House for the improvement of navigation on the River Clyde. The numerous shoals and sandbanks made it possible for only very small ships to sail right up to Glasgow, so that most goods were transported overland from Port Glasgow or Greenock. The motion was approved. The expenditure was met by the merchants and the ship owners. John's initiative contributed greatly to the growth of Glasgow as a major port.

Apart from being a leading tobacco merchant, John McCall was one of the six original partners, mostly *Tobacco Lords,* of the aristocratic Thistle Bank, which commenced business in 1761 with a capital of £7,000. The legal name of the bank was Maxwell, Ritchie & Company, but it was commonly known as The Thistle Bank, which name was derived from the emblem of a thistle which appeared on the bank's notes. The bank operated for 75 years until it merged in 1836 with the Glasgow Union Banking Company, the forerunner of the Union Bank of Scotland, then of the Bank of Scotland, HBOS and finally the Lloyds Banking Group.

In 1760 John purchased 25 acres of land and salmon fishing rights on the River Clyde at Bridgeton, two miles east of Glasgow, where he authorised the construction of a country mansion known as *Belvidere*. The estate was bounded on the east by the lands of Westthorn and on the west by those of Springbank. The Clyde skirts the property to the south. John and his family had the pleasure of living in style in this grand house with its extensive grounds for the next 25 years until he died in 1790.

Belvidere was sold in 1791, the year after John McCall's death, to his son-in-law, Robert McNair, a sugar refiner, whose family had made a fortune from the sugar business. The old house was demolished in 1887 after the land had been acquired by the Glasgow Board of Health for use as a hospital "*for fever and other infectious diseases*". *Belvidere* became a general geriatric hospital before it closed in 1999. The land has since been redeveloped as an upmarket housing estate, while wrought iron gates still mark the entrance to the old house.

Then, in 1775 John arranged the building of the *Black House*, a handsome mansion which formerly stood at the corner of Queen Street and Argyle Street. According to the 19th century historian Robert Reid, John McCall's house was a square house with a pavilion roof and a double stair with a handsome iron railing jutting out on to Westergate (now Argyle Street) and had more than forty windows - a very large number for the period. Reid noted that the mansion had *an almost ink-black appearance*, which he put down to the fact that it was built with stone from the Black Quarry. This quarry was located near North Woodside Road and produced the stone for Glasgow buildings from the mid-17th century until it became exhausted at the end of the 18th century. Reid also claimed that it was McCall who was responsible for having the traditional name, Cow Loan, changed to the more sophisticated Queen Street. McCall's family sold the house after his death and it was demolished in about 1815 to make room for a tenement building, which itself was later pulled down and is now the site of a busy thoroughfare.

Like his father he married twice. By his first wife, Margaret Craufurd, he had no issue. But he married again, in 1764 at the age of 49, Helen Cross, daughter of another Glasgow merchant, Robert Cross, whose ancestors included both a Dean of Guild and a Lord Provost.

At the time of the American War of Independence, many Glasgow merchants suffered financial failure as the tobacco trade virtually came to an end. After hostilities broke out in 1775, the tobacco trade shrunk such that by 1780 it was at 6% of the pre-war level. Many *Tobacco Lords* had lent large sums to the planters in Maryland and Virginia to develop their estates and the total of such debts was estimated to be over £1.3million. Much of this was irrecoverable. However those who had built up large tobacco stocks in Glasgow sold them for a large profit. One tobacco merchant, William Cunninghame, made an even greater fortune. At the outbreak of war, Cunninghame's business partners possessed large stocks of tobacco which they had purchased for around three pence per pound. After the war began and trade was disrupted, the price of tobacco rose. Cunninghame's partners, confident that the rebellious colonists would soon be defeated, sold their stock at sixpence per pound. Cunninghame took the opposite view and he purchased their entire stock. Eventually, as the long war disrupted supplies, the price of tobacco rose to 3 shillings and sixpence, making Cunninghame a huge fortune.

John McCall was a staunch royalist and in 1783 he suffered considerable loss and forfeiture of his estates and loans in Virginia as a result of his adherence to the British Crown during the War of Independence. He received some, but insufficient, compensation from the British Government - poor recompense for his loyalty. This is confirmed by a list of the addresses of the Merchant Elite in Glasgow contained in John Tait's *Directory for the City of Glasgow*, 1783, in which John's name is conspicuous by its absence. He died at the *Black House* in 1790 and was buried in the family vault in the High Churchyard of Glasgow Cathedral.

John had four sons and six daughters by his marriage to Helen Cross, all born in Glasgow:
- Sarah McCall, born 29 August 1765. On 30 November 1786, she married Alexander Bonar, a banker of Edinburgh, son of the Reverend John Bonar, minister of Perth. She died in 1835
- Margaret McCall, born 4 August 1766. She married at Belvidere on 25 September 1786, James Spreull, of Spreulls Land, a merchant in Glasgow. She died in 1836
- Helen McCall, born 25 August 1767 She married on 21 December 1789 Robert McNair, who acquired Belvidere on her father's death
- Samuel McCall, born 16 September 1769. After completing his studies in Glasgow, he sailed in 1787, when barely eighteen years of age, for Virginia. After a short while he moved to Limerick, where he continued his merchanting business and died there on 2 May 1805. He married on 10 October 1799 Margaret Wallace, daughter of William Wallace, a merchant in Limerick, who survived her husband by as many as 57 years, dying in Glasgow in 1862, where she was buried in the Cathedral Vault
- John McCall, born 1 April, 1771. He emigrated to the West Indies, where he died unmarried at Castries on the Island of Santa Lucia on 3 February 1821

Children of John McCall and Helen Cross

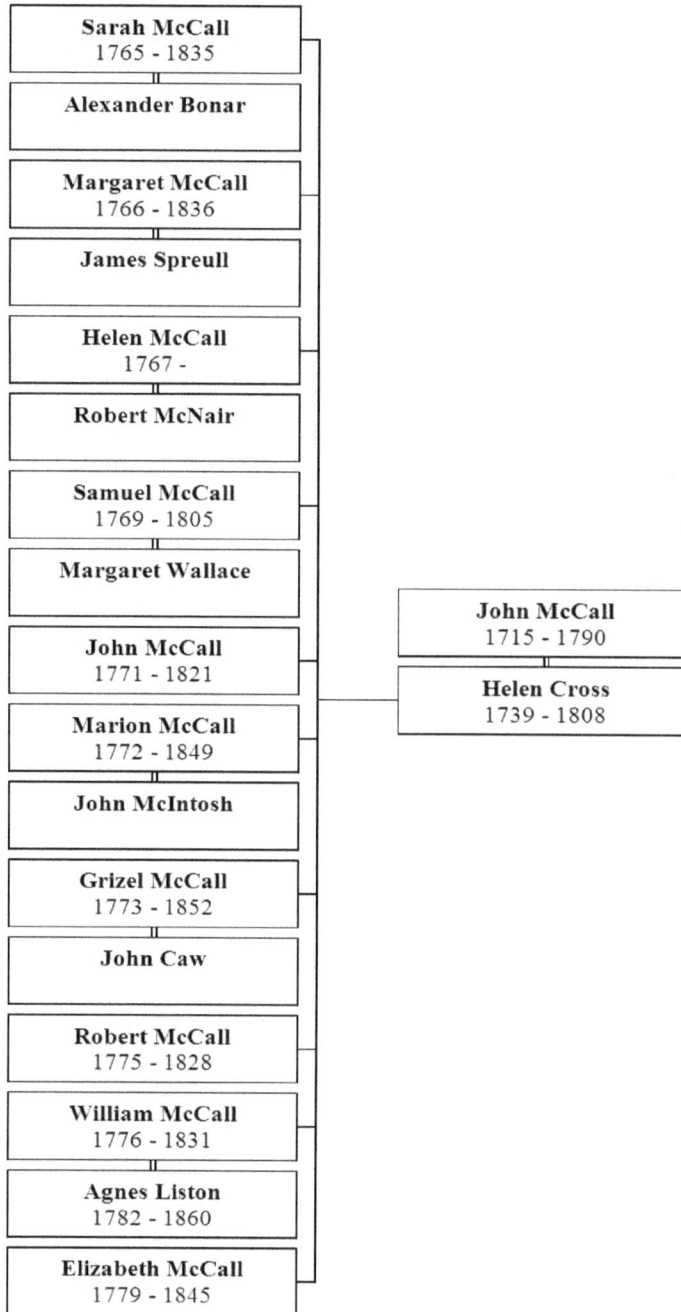

Sarah McCall 1765 - 1835	
Alexander Bonar	
Margaret McCall 1766 - 1836	
James Spreull	
Helen McCall 1767 -	
Robert McNair	
Samuel McCall 1769 - 1805	
Margaret Wallace	
John McCall 1771 - 1821	**John McCall** 1715 - 1790
Marion McCall 1772 - 1849	**Helen Cross** 1739 - 1808
John McIntosh	
Grizel McCall 1773 - 1852	
John Caw	
Robert McCall 1775 - 1828	
William McCall 1776 - 1831	
Agnes Liston 1782 - 1860	
Elizabeth McCall 1779 - 1845	

- Marion McCall, born 24 May 1772. She married in 1812 John McIntosh of Glasgow and died in 1849
- Grizel McCall, born 23 September 1773. On 3 September 1799 she married John Caw, a merchant, later Provost of Perth, where she died on 27 January 1852
- Robert McCall, born 16 May 1775, who died unmarried in 1828
- William McCall, born 13 October 1776 (see below)
- Elizabeth McCall, born 19 January 1779 and died unmarried in 1845.

The two eldest sons who survived their father became merchants in Limerick, Ireland and Saint Lucia respectively. A fourth son, William McCall, of whom more anon, was born in Glasgow in 1776 just as the storm clouds were looming.

By the last quarter of the 18th century, Glasgow's position as the major entrepôt for tobacco trading had been severely challenged. The trading ties with Virginia and Maryland had been cut as a result of the American War of Independence. But, in its place, trade with the West Indies increased, with Glasgow merchants exporting finished cloths and other goods and importing sugar and cotton. By 1800 Glasgow was Britain's biggest importer of sugar. Trade with the Baltic countries, in flax and wood, developed and then with Canada after more Scottish families emigrated there. As the 19th century progressed, Glasgow became a hub for the growing major manufacturing and shipbuilding industries.

As for tobacco, Bristol, the UK's historical tobacco trading port, resumed its role as the major importer and then engaged in cigarette manufacture for which it became well known, through companies such as Wills & Watkins (later WD & HO Wills) and, still later, Imperial Tobacco.

The fortunes of the extended McCall family varied greatly. Those who had emigrated to North America had, with a few exceptions, become prosperous merchants and thrived in the newly independent country. John's cousin, James McCall (1788-1866) remained in Glasgow and became a successful wine merchant purchasing the Daldowie estate in 1830 and leaving £141,945 on his death in September 1866. But poor John McCall lost all his lands in Maryland and Virginia. He had debts owing to him by Virginians in 1776. His two houses, the *Black House* and *Belvidere,* were both sold after his death in 1790. After many years, his heirs received a certain amount from the Government. However, with a large family, including four surviving sons, to share the estate, his successors inherited lesser wealth than their father and grandfather had enjoyed.

Was this a case of rags to riches and back to rags in the three generations? Well not quite rags, as our story will reveal. But it does show how easily wealth which has been carefully accumulated through industry and good fortune can be so easily dissipated through external political and economic factors, bad timing, and having a large family. Our next chapter relates another such experience.

But, before that, the story of Archibald McCall, John's youngest brother, merits telling as it highlights the difficulties caused by the American War of Independence to a member of the McCall family who had emigrated to the Colony.

Archibald McCall (1734-1814)

In developing his tobacco merchanting business, Samuel McCall needed to have members of the family to be resident in Virginia to interface with local planters and to purchase tobacco and store it before shipment to Glasgow. By 1754, both James, Samuel McCall's third son, and Archibald, his youngest son, lived in Essex County, Virginia. James purchased land for their father in Piscataway Creek, where a warehouse had been constructed, and renamed *New Glasgow*. James returned to Scotland in 1757 leaving Archibald in charge of the family's affairs. Archibald also established his own business in Tappahannock, buying land on the Rappahannock River where, in 1763, he built *McCall House*, which still stands today.

He married Catherine Flood, an heiress from Farnham, Richmond County, but she died in 1767 shortly after the birth of their second daughter. After a dispute over, in his own words, "*pecuniary transactions*" with his father-in-law, Archibald decided that, as a widower, it would be preferable for his two young daughters to be brought up in Scotland where his own family lived, and he sent them there in 1773. Archibald had significant business interests in Virginia: a farm of 502 acres for growing corn, a granary on a tributary of Hoskins Creek, a flour mill and a bakery. He operated ships in Chesapeake Bay as well as being the agent for the family's business in Scotland. It took Archibald longer than he anticipated to sell or to settle his businesses in America. Then war broke out in April 1775. Expecting the troubles to be over within a few months, he put all his affairs in the hands of William Shedden, his partner and manager, and his young cousin, George McCall. However, Shedden was ordered out of the country in January 1777, as a "*Royalist sympathiser*". This left George, who was described in a Court judgement in March 1777 as "*uniformly friendly to the cause of American liberty*" with power of attorney to look after Archibald's businesses and property.

The war was to last eight years (from 1775 to 1783) during which time George wrote to Archibald pleading with him to return to Virginia to save his estates from confiscation. Archibald responded asking for a passport to be issued to enable him to travel to Essex County. However travel was not possible as the British Parliament has passed a law restricting free passage to the erstwhile colonies. Correspondence between the two had to be sent indirectly via the French West Indies. Further, Archibald's elder daughter had died and he did not want to risk the health of his younger daughter. To make matters worse, in an effort to secure an income, he had formed an underwriting business in London in which he lost a great deal when his partner died. He was in debt to his former partner's family and, as a consequence, he was obliged to pledge his possessions in Tappahannock as security.

When the American war ended in 1783 Archibald McCall chartered a vessel and sailed with his surviving daughter, Katherine ("*Katty*" or "*Kitty*"), for Virginia, seeking to recover his possessions in Essex County and those in Richmond County left by his father-in-law. In 1787, his cousin George brought a legal claim for remuneration owed to him as a result of his management of the McCall business affairs and in saving Archibald's property during the war. The Essex County court ruled in favour of George but Archibald appealed to the General Court. In 1789, Archibald transferred his Essex County properties, including his home in Tappahannock to the heirs of his former partner in the London underwriting business. He lost his possessions but moved, with his daughter, to his deceased wife's family property, *Cedar Grove*, in Richmond County, where he died in 1814. Allegedly the ghost of Katherine has been seen many times at their former Tappahannock home "*dressed in white*".

A McCall Merchant in Liverpool in the 19th Century

William McCall (1776 – 1831)

Moving away from home and travelling to faraway places in search of work and opportunity had become natural to the McCalls as to many other English and Scottish families in the 18th and 19th centuries.

William was John McCall's fourth (and youngest) son. Over the previous three generations, there had been a history of McCall siblings establishing businesses in other locations. His two elder brothers, Samuel and John, were merchants in Limerick and Saint Lucia respectively. His uncles, George and Archibald, had merchanting businesses in Virginia. And his great uncle, George, and George's nephew, Samuel, had emigrated to Philadelphia where they were pillars of the local community.

William's father and grandfather had prospered as a result of Glasgow's tobacco trade. But, when this came under pressure and was threatened after the American War of Independence, young William did what his grandfather had done before him, he *"got on his bike"*, to use the advice and slogan coined by Lord (Norman) Tebbit in the UK in the 1980's.

At an early age, William travelled to Liverpool to take advantage of the city's growth and began merchanting, a trade he knew well.

Liverpool's geographical position at the head of the Mersey Estuary on the north-west coast of England was well suited to take advantage of trade with North America and the rest of the world. As the neighbouring, and ancient, port of Chester declined through the silting up of the River Dee, Liverpool took its place. Liverpool's first trade with the Americas occurred in the mid-17th century and developed further after the restoration to the throne of Charles II in 1660. Tobacco, cotton and sugar were imported and exchanged for exports such as textiles, coal and salt as well as copper, brass and guns. At the turn of the century, the triangular slave trade began between Liverpool, West Africa, the West Indies and back to Liverpool, taking advantage of the trade winds and ocean currents. In 1715, the first dry dock was constructed, with a capacity of 100 ships. This ensured that, despite 10 metre tides, the 4th highest in the world, the ships were in a safe, water filled harbour. They did not need to anchor in the middle of the River Mersey or on sand banks at low tide. Loading and unloading was made easy. In time, four more docks were constructed.

By 1800, Liverpool had the third largest registered tonnage of shipping in Great Britain. 40% of the world's and 80% of Britain's Atlantic slave activity was accounted for by slave ships from Liverpool. The city was linked to Manchester via a canal, completed in 1721 and extended to Leeds in 1816. Hospitals, schools and a new town hall were built. Then, in 1807, *The Abolition of the Slave Trade Act* was passed, banning the slave trade in the British Empire. Liverpool's wealth from this trade had led to the city's prosperity and had stimulated trading and industrial manufacture in the North West of England and the Midlands. Its place, post 1807, was taken by the growing cotton and textile trade which became a hallmark of Lancashire's economic success in the 19th and early 20th centuries.

Children of William McCall & Agnes Liston

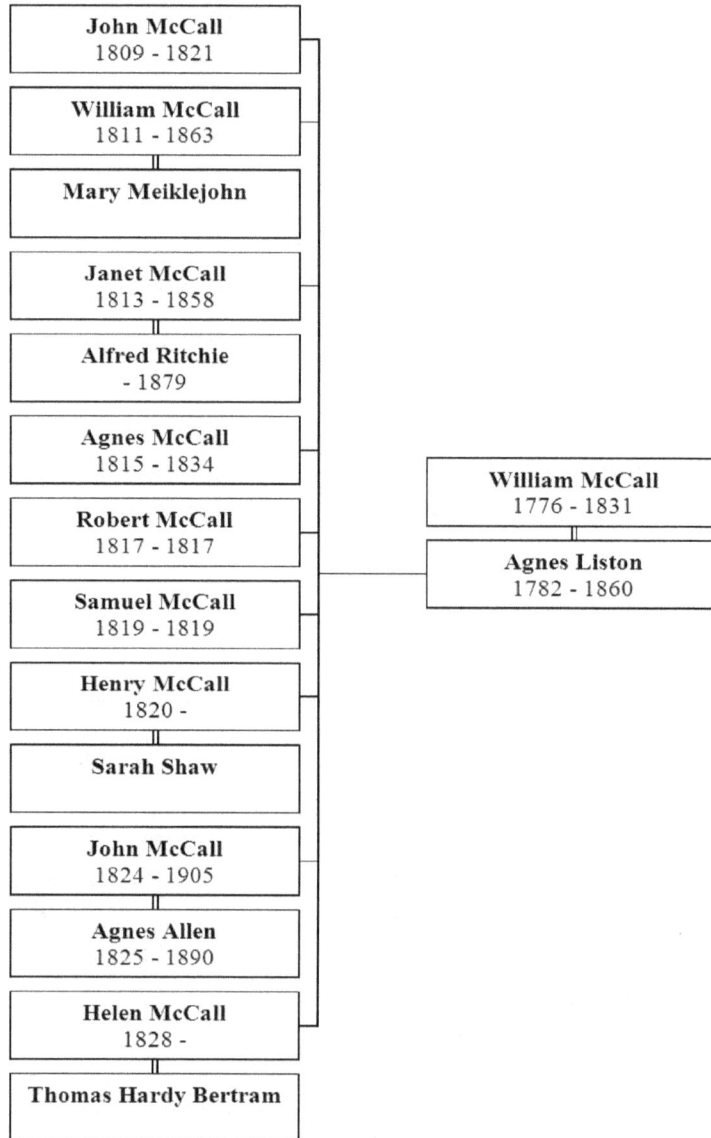

```
┌─────────────────────────┐
│      John McCall         │
│      1809 - 1821         │
├─────────────────────────┤
│     William McCall       │
│      1811 - 1863         │
├─────────────────────────┤
│     Mary Meiklejohn      │
├─────────────────────────┤
│      Janet McCall        │
│      1813 - 1858         │
├─────────────────────────┤
│     Alfred Ritchie       │
│        - 1879            │
├─────────────────────────┤
│      Agnes McCall        │
│      1815 - 1834         │
├─────────────────────────┤
│     Robert McCall        │
│      1817 - 1817         │
├─────────────────────────┤
│     Samuel McCall        │
│      1819 - 1819         │
├─────────────────────────┤
│      Henry McCall        │
│      1820 -              │
├─────────────────────────┤
│      Sarah Shaw          │
├─────────────────────────┤
│      John McCall         │
│      1824 - 1905         │
├─────────────────────────┤
│      Agnes Allen         │
│      1825 - 1890         │
├─────────────────────────┤
│      Helen McCall        │
│      1828 -              │
├─────────────────────────┤
│  Thomas Hardy Bertram    │
└─────────────────────────┘
```

┌─────────────────────────┐
│   William McCall   │
│   1776 - 1831   │
├─────────────────────────┤
│   Agnes Liston   │
│   1782 - 1860   │
└─────────────────────────┘

When William McCall began his merchanting business in Liverpool in the first decade of the 19th century, the city's population had grown to around 78,000, marginally smaller than Glasgow's 84,000. There had been a large influx of migrants from Wales and Ireland as well as immigrants from Scandinavia and Holland. The majority of the population was not native to the city. Liverpool had become a very international city. To demonstrate this and Liverpool's growing importance, the world's first American consul, John Maury, was posted to the city in 1790.

By 1821, the population had reached 118,000 as a result of the high birth rate and also from Irish immigration, prompted by the potato famines which became worse as the 19th century progressed. By 1831, the city's population had grown further to 165,000. The growth gave business opportunities for everyone and Liverpool's position as a port and centre of maritime activity eclipsed all but London.

Liverpool was also becoming a very gracious Regency city, with fine new houses, parks and other amenities. In 1772, the Theatre Royal had been opened in Williamson Square. A new town hall was constructed between 1795 and 1820. In 1797, the Atheneum was founded with its building completed in 1799 as a centre for literary activity. In 1802, the Botanical Gardens were opened. Work began in 1811 on St Luke's Church. Then, in 1817, gas was introduced to light the street lamps. And, to demonstrate the city's importance as a commercial centre, the Bank of England opened a branch in Liverpool in 1827.

William McCall was a contributor to this expanding commercial and economic activity. He developed a successful merchanting business. Then, in 1808, William married Agnes Liston, daughter of the Rev Robert Liston of Aberdour. Despite his move to Liverpool, he had not lost his Scottish ties and the Listons were a very distinguished Scottish family.

William and Agnes lived at Parkside, at that time a spacious suburb of Liverpool with parks and genteel Regency houses near Sefton Park and Wavertree. They had five children who survived their youth, namely:
- William McCall, born 14 May 1811 in Liverpool. He married Mary Meiklejohn and died in Clifton, Bristol in November 1863 leaving two sons and three daughters
- Janet McCall, born 21 January 1813 in Liverpool. She married Alfred Ritchie (perhaps a descendant of the Glasgow Ritchies who were *Tobacco Lords*?) in Greenwich and lived later in Stroud. She died in 1858 leaving two sons and six daughters
- Henry McCall, born 30 July 1820 at Maiden Hill, of which more below. He married Sarah Shaw, moved to Westbourne in Hampshire and had one daughter
- John McCall, born 22 June 1824 at Maiden Hill (see below)
- Helen McCall, born 7 June 1828, who married Thomas Hardy Bertram, and lived in Beckenham, Kent.

As the slave trade was ending, the Napoleonic Wars (1803-1815) brought further opportunities for those engaged in merchanting. First, British soldiers needed victuals as well as guns and ammunition. Liverpool's merchant fleet was well placed to assist the British Army as it fought in the Spanish Netherlands, the Iberian Peninsula, France and Belgium. Then, protected by the Royal Navy, particularly after Nelson's victory at Trafalgar in 1805, Britain's share of international trade increased while that of France decreased.

William McCall
(1776 – 1831)

Wellington's victory at Waterloo in 1815 confirmed Great Britain's role as the dominant European power and the leading world trader.

Available statistics of the number ships in Liverpool in the first two decades of the 19th century show the increase in activity as a result of supplying military campaigns and in the years following the defeat of Napoleon:

1800	4,746
1805	4,618
1815	6,440
1822	8,136
1824	10,001

William McCall took advantage of these opportunities and his merchanting business flourished. In the words of Bertram Hardy McCall, the biographer of the McCall family, *"He went to Liverpool where he was a merchant during the early years of his life, and by some fortunate commercial enterprises at the time of the Duke of Wellington's wars, rendered himself independent of professional occupation, when quite a young man."*

Then, in 1813 he did what his father and grandfather had done before him. After succeeding in business, he spent his hard earned money on property and acquired, from the Commissioners of the Crown, an estate of 275 acres at Maiden Hill, a few miles north of Penrith. It was barren forest land when he bought it and he built the house, which still stands, and lived there for about 12 years. His concept was to make the place a sort of *model farm*, with the latest machinery and equipment. He spent much time and large sums of money on improving the estate to make the land more productive. Perhaps he was too enthusiastic and overly pioneering in his endeavours. In any event, he cannot be said to have succeeded, for Maiden Hill, which cost him in one way and another as much as £40,000, was sold after his death for less than a quarter of that sum.

Perhaps William was ahead of his time. The Industrial Revolution had heralded some very exciting inventions. Just a few years later, in 1830, George Stephenson drove his Rocket, named the *Northumbrian*, at the opening of the Liverpool and Manchester Railway. Steam powered ploughing machines and portable threshing machines were introduced into some farms in the 1850's. Sadly, while William had sensed the potential opportunities presented by growing mechanisation, it seems as though he got the timing wrong.

In the summer of 1825, William let his farming estate in Cumberland and he went back to live in Liverpool at Parkside. He also built some houses in Falkner Street, into one of which his widow moved with her children, after his death, and she lived there for several years. Falkner Street is close to the city centre in an area with attractive squares.

In the spring of 1831 William went with his family to stay at Beaumaris for the benefit of his health, which had been in a delicate state, and he died there of a heart attack while driving in his carriage, aged 54. He was buried in St. James' Cemetery, Liverpool.

William McCall had great physical strength in his younger days and was tall. He was considered, by friends and colleagues alike, to be a man of the highest integrity and good character, of a placid and quiet disposition, and exceedingly polished and refined in his manners and address to all with whom he came in contact.

In Lesley Stuttard's possession is an image of William in the form of a silhouette of the profile of his face and shoulders. He is wearing a high cravat wrapped tightly around his neck and a ruffled jabot protruding above his waistcoat. He looks quite dapper.

William McCall had been a successful merchant, making a great deal of money as a young man. But, yet again, a McCall had lost a significant portion of his wealth – in this case through a seemingly over ambitious development of a *model farm*. In hindsight, it is possible that William knew more about merchanting than farming.

It was time for the next generation of McCalls to *"get on their bike"*.

London, then South America and Australia, beckoned as places of business opportunity. The McCalls were yet again on the move.

The McCalls' Meat Business in London and South America

John McCall (1824 – 1905)

John McCall was William's third son. Born at Maiden Hill, he was brought up by his widowed mother in Liverpool. He trained as a civil engineer and practised this profession in Liverpool and in Manchester after he moved there in 1845.

His sister Janet, who was nine years older than John, married Alfred Ritchie (perhaps a descendant of the Ritchies who had been Glasgow *Tobacco Lords*). The McCall family knew the Ritchie family well, as co-investors in the Thistle Bank in Glasgow in 1761. John McCall's grandfather, also John, had been a partner with James Ritchie in the bank. As *Tobacco Lords*, they were fellow merchants who both enjoyed the Virginia trade. One can imagine, although it is not proven, that the families kept in touch after they left Glasgow. Janet McCall met Alfred Ritchie, perhaps through their parents' introduction, and they married in Greenwich in 1840.

Also (perhaps in the 1840's?) in the days when it was fashionable for young men to complete their education by embarking on a *grand tour*, John McCall's brother-in-law Alfred Ritchie accompanied John on a visit to South America. The introduction, via the parents or through Janet, may well have been the link that brought John and Alfred together to travel on their *grand tour*.

At that time, the flat grasslands of Uruguay and Argentine bordering the River Plate supported enormous numbers of cattle which were raised mainly for their hides. The animals were butchered in small yards, known as *saladeros*, scattered around the rural areas. The best parts of the meat were salted and sun-dried. They were then sold to Brazil as *charqui* or *zarque* or *jerky*. The fats, in the form of tallow, were used for producing soap. While visiting the yards, our two travellers observed that, along with the entrails, the tongues were being thrown away. They concluded that this was a missed business opportunity and that it would be profitable to put the tongues to better use. Later, when they and their respective families were engaged in meat preservation and canning, South America proved to be a lucrative source of raw material and of canning ox tongues, as our story will reveal.

In Manchester John McCall had married Agnes Allan, daughter of Robert Allan, FRS of Edinburgh, in April 1847 at Manchester Cathedral. Family lore has it that Agnes was a descendant of *Barbara Allan*, the subject of the 18th century song.

John and Agnes had five children who survived their childhood:
- William McCall, born in 1851 in Greenwich, Kent (see further below)
- John McCall, born in 1854 in Greenwich, Kent and died young in 1870
- Janet Sophia McCall, born in 1859 in Walthamstow, Essex. She married Ransome Wallis and became a philanthropist and was founder of the Mission of Hope
- Hardy Bertram McCall, born on 1 December 1859 in Walthamstow, Essex. He wrote many books, including two on the McCall family history (see further below)
- Allan (known as "*Tatto*") McCall, born on 19 November 1861 in Walthamstow, Essex (see further below).

Children of John McCall & Agnes Allan

```
┌─────────────────────────┐
│    William McCall        │
│    1851 - 1929           │
└─────────────────────────┘
┌─────────────────────────┐
│ Leonora Emily Walter     │
│ Basden Whittingham       │
└─────────────────────────┘
┌─────────────────────────┐
│    John McCall           │
│    1854 - 1870           │
└─────────────────────────┘
┌─────────────────────────┐        ┌─────────────────────────┐
│  Janet Sophia McCall     │        │    John McCall           │
│    1859 -                │        │    1824 - 1905           │
└─────────────────────────┘        └─────────────────────────┘
┌─────────────────────────┐        ┌─────────────────────────┐
│    Ransome Wallis        │        │    Agnes Allen           │
│                          │        │    1825 - 1890           │
└─────────────────────────┘        └─────────────────────────┘
┌─────────────────────────┐
│  Hardy Bertram McCall    │
│    1859 - 1934           │
└─────────────────────────┘
┌─────────────────────────┐
│  Vida-Mary Anderson      │
│                          │
└─────────────────────────┘
┌─────────────────────────┐
│    Allan McCall          │
│    1861 - 1935           │
└─────────────────────────┘
┌─────────────────────────┐
│ Ruth Helen Shoobridge    │
│    1860 - 1947           │
└─────────────────────────┘
```

In 1851, like many of his forebears, John McCall sought opportunity elsewhere, moving from Manchester to London at the age of 27. Living initially in Greenwich near his sister Janet, he collaborated with Samuel Sextus Ritchie, also of Greenwich, and perhaps a younger brother of his brother-in-law, Alfred. Samuel Ritchie and John McCall established a meat canning factory in Houndsditch using the calcium chloride brine method of preservation. Under the name, Ritchie & McCall, they won medals at the Great Exhibition of 1851 and their plant was commented on favourably at the time of the Royal Navy canned meat scandal, of which more below. *The Illustrated London News* of 31 January 1852 included a photograph entitled *"General view of kitchen at Richie* (sic) *& McCall's Cannery, Houndsditch, London, 1852"*.

RITCHIE AND M'CALL'S PRESERVED MEAT ESTABLISHMENT, HOUNDSDITCH.—THE KITCHEN.—(SEE NEXT PAGE.)

As a method of preserving food, canning had been around for some time. Originally discovered by a Frenchman, Philippe de Girard, it was patented in England by his agent, Peter Durand, in 1810, using the technique of boiling the food in the can and then sealing it. The patent was sold to Bryan Donkin who commenced canning food from his factory in Bermondsey, in East London. In 1813, the Admiralty bought 156 lbs of Donkin's food, which was enjoyed by officers and sailors alike, as it was tastier than salted or dried beef. From then, sales of canned meat by Donkin to the Royal Navy increased and supplies were particularly sought after for the Arctic expeditions. Donkin was joined by John Gamble, who succeeded him and who also commenced operations in 1830 in Cork in the Republic of Ireland, where there was a ready supply of raw material and where labour was cheaper. By 1824, the patent had expired and other food processors began supplying the Royal Navy with canned food. At the Great Exhibition of 1851, Gamble displayed his canning wares and it was clear that the concept was gaining public favour. But, there was a temporary hiccup in the development of the canning industry.

Samuel Sextus Ritchie was roughly the same age as his business partner, John McCall, but was described as the senior partner, perhaps because of his knowledge of the process of canning. Richie & McCall became the London agent of Stefan Goldner, a Hungarian who owned a canning factory in Moldavia, Romania. Mr Goldner had won contracts supplying the Royal Navy and also the ill-fated expedition in search of the North West Passage by HMS Terror and HMS Erebus under the command of Sir John Franklin. But Goldner's products became increasingly defective. The quality control over his production was extremely poor. A Parliamentary Select Committee Enquiry in 1852 on Preserved Meats (Navy) criticised Goldner and, by implication, Ritchie, as a result of which he was banned from tendering for Navy rations. Goldner's business ceased and Ritchie emigrated to Australia in 1856.

This left John McCall to continue the London business which he renamed McCall & Co, Preserved Provision Merchants, trading also under the name of John McCall & Co, from 137 Houndsditch. The company developed innovative technology for preserving and canning beef, mutton, tongues, vegetables and soups. The Goldner incident must have made a mark on John McCall, then in his late twenties, and showed him the importance of quality control in canning. He expanded his business in the UK and then in South America and he acted as the distributor of preserved meat supplied by Australian companies who used his technology. But, he was always concerned to ensure that his products were safe for human consumption and this obsession was to stand him in good stead as his business expanded.

Stefan Goldner was born in Hungary around 1810 and moved to London in 1837, his profession being described as merchant. He filed a patent in 1841 for the use of brine rather than water as the boiling agent in the canning process, so that the temperature at which the product was cooked was higher. In 1845, he won contracts for canned meat with the Royal Navy by cost cutting, using cheap labour at a factory he established in Galatz, Moldavia, where there was also a ready supply of raw material. His contracts with the Navy increased. When Goldner was pressed by the Admiralty to deliver greater quantities of his products he tried to do this by increasing the size of his cans from 4 lbs or 6 lbs to 9 lbs and even to 32 lbs. But there were complaints about the food in the cans going off. In 1852 an inspection by the Navy's meat inspectors found that most of the larger cans delivered to the Portsmouth Victualling Yard and elsewhere contained rotten, putrid meat not fit for human consumption. Reports by the Inspectors revealed that most of the bad meat was contained in the cans of 9 lbs and 32 lbs, while almost no bad meat was found in the smaller cans of 6 lbs and under. It seems that the heating apparatus available at that time was not powerful enough to sterilise the meat in the centre of the larger containers.

It was reported that more than 600,000 lbs of Goldner's meat (to a value of almost £6,700) had to be thrown away. It was also revealed that Goldner had signed a contract with Sir John Franklin to supply him with 8,000 tins of soups, meat and vegetables for his expedition in 1845 to explore the North West Passage. As the deadline for sailing approached, Goldner realised that he would have to provide the food in larger tins which should have required longer cooking times. Goldner did not do this and, as a result, the food was not properly cooked and also not properly sealed. This caused bacteria and, possibly lead poisoning. It is also alleged that Goldner used spoiled food in the processing of this and other contracts. Some historians have suggested that the lead poisoning in the bones found of Franklin's crew was due to the poor quality of manufacture of the tins, allowing lead to penetrate the contents. However, others have argued that the lead poisoning was more likely to have been caused by the lead water pipes in the two ships.

When the report of the 1852 Parliamentary Enquiry was published, Goldner was severely censured. The public's reaction to the findings and to canned food was very negative. But this concern soon subsided and the concept of buying preserved food in cans became even more popular in Great Britain in the 1860's.

The policy of John McCall & Co was to buy produce when prices were low. Thus the products they made varied from week to week depending on availability and prices. Canning became an accepted method of preserving food as the variety increased and with greater quality control.

After Samuel Ritchie left for Australia, John McCall entered into partnership with someone by the name of Frederick Peel, but they parted company, as recorded in *The London Gazette* of July 4, 1862: "*Notice is hereby given, that the Partnership heretofore subsisting between us the undersigned, John McCall and Frederick Peel, of No. 137, Houndsditch, in the city of London, as Preserved Provision Merchants, carrying on business under the firm of John McCall and Co, was this day dissolved by mutual consent.—As witness our hands, this 31st day of March, 1862. John McCall. Fred. Peel.*"

Meantime, in 1856, John McCall moved with his family from Greenwich to Walthamstow then a gracious rural suburb of London. Taking advantage of the significant earnings from his successful business, he acquired a substantial house, *Woodlands*. *Whites Trade Directory* records John McCall as living there in 1863 and Hardy Bertram McCall in his book *Memoirs of My Ancestors – A Collection of Genealogical Memoranda Respecting Several Old Scottish Families*, 1884 includes an illustration of *Woodlands* in 1865.

Woodlands in 1865.

In the International Exhibition of 1862 John McCall & Co (with John McCall as the sole owner) is listed in the Illustrated Catalogue as No 802 described as "*Preserved provisions*".

Also in 1862, perhaps at the suggestion of Ritchie, who had emigrated to Australia in 1856 in the wake of the Goldner scandal, John McCall sought to patent his canning technology in Australia. The Victoria Government Gazette of Friday 5 December 1862 records the following gazetted under Applications for Patents for Inventions: "*John McCall, of Houndsditch, in the city of London, provision merchant, and Bevan George Sloper, of Walthamstow, in the county of Essex, England, chemist, have applied for a patent for **An improvement in the preservation of articles of food**, and have deposited their specification at this office, on the 17th day of November, 1862*".

In 1863 a cattle plague (rinderpest) broke out in England and spread rapidly across the whole country. This became so widespread that it created a serious shortage of beef in the years 1865 to 1867. The demand for food to cater for the growing population of Great Britain added to the shortage and resulted in a global search for meat which was satisfied initially by imports from Australia and then, in the 1870's, from South America.

The statistics of UK imports of canned meat from Australia show a staggering increase:

1867	286,528 lbs
1868	878,444 lbs
1869	2,000,000 lbs
1880	16,000,000 lbs

Samuel Ritchie began his new life in Australian as a partner in a wine and spirit merchanting venture. Then, in 1867, perhaps prompted by the demand from the UK, he decided to return to meat canning. He was appointed the manager of the Melbourne Meat Preserving Company, which he grew to become the largest and most successful of the Australian meat preserving companies. The technology used in this factory and in most other successful meat canning factories in Australia in the 19th century was that derived from Goldner via the Ritchie & McCall firm in 137 Houndsditch. Using the contact with his former partner, Ritchie arranged for John McCall & Co to import and distribute the product of the Melbourne Meat Preserving Company and, in 1870, John McCall & Co sold 38,000 cases of preserved meat obtained from this supplier. Samuel Ritchie died in Australia in 1879.

An Englishman, Charles Tindal, who had emigrated to Australia, formed the Australian Meat Company, after visiting the UK to study canning, and the company's address was shown as 137 Houndsditch. John McCall & Co also acted as the London agents from 1867 but later the Australian Meat Company established its own offices in London.
In *Chemical News and Journal of Physical Science* of 1873, the editor William Crookes describes, in a chapter on London's International Exhibition of 1873, "McCall & Co exhibited meat from Uruguay, some kangaroo tail soup, and indeed *kangaroo a la mode*, and in every other mode. This firm also exhibited dried turtle for the making of real turtle soup".

Refrigeration was gradually being introduced, starting in the 1870's, as a means of preserving meat for transportation to Europe and North America. Canning companies came under threat or else they embraced improved means of preserving meat. But, despite the advent of refrigeration, canning had become a tried and tested means of transporting preserved meat and it was cheaper. While some Australian canning companies suffered in the short term from refrigeration, canning technology also improved. By 1880, the UK was importing 16 million lbs of canned meat from Australia. Canning companies sprang up around the globe, using railways and roads that were being constructed at a rapid pace.

Building on its success in canning in Houndsditch and acting as distributor for Australian imports, McCall & Co then developed a thriving meat canning business in South America. The geographical expansion to Argentina, Uruguay and Brazil was undertaken mainly by John McCall's eldest son, William, and, later, with help from William's younger brother Allan. William also became Chairman of McCall & Co and inherited *Woodlands* (which was later demolished in 1890) from his father in 1879.

John McCall's business thrived as the demand for canned food increased. In 1884, contributing greatly to the interests of his trade, he was elected Chairman of the

ENGLISH MANUFACTURERS AT THE PARIS EXHIBITION.

THE PICTORIAL WORLD.

DECEMBER 21st, 1878.

269

MESSRS. M'CALL's EXHIBIT OF PRESERVED MEAT.

"Preserved Food Trades' Section" of the London Chamber of Commerce & Industry ("LCCI") which had been formed in 1881. He held this position for over 20 years until 1903. The section's role seems to have been particularly concerned with defending the interests of the preserved food trade, which seems to have been held responsible, at least in the public mind, for fatalities alleged to result from eating canned foods. Being a leading preserved food merchant, John McCall was anxious to see high standards maintained in the food industry and, as early as 1884, the section he chaired was calling for clear food labelling and for practical advice, such as removing the contents from cans once they had been opened. Its interests were national and not confined to London.

John McCall became a man of substance. He was a leading figure in the Evangelical Movement of the 19th century, much inspired by the American Evangelists, Moody and Sankey, and their songs. He was also a friend of Lord Shaftesbury, the great Christian statesman and philanthropist. John's wife, Agnes, died in 1890 and John died in December 1905 in Epsom, Surrey.

William McCall (1851 – 1929)

John McCall's eldest son, William, was born in Greenwich. He was privately educated and then spent time at Lausanne University. In 1869 he married Leonora Whittingham, by whom he had four daughters.

Encouraged by his father, William was the driver behind the expansion of the firm in South America, first in Paysandu in Uruguay, then to a limited extent in Argentina, and finally in Brazil (Bage and Tupancireta). Their main product was canned ox tongue, which became extremely popular. It was marketed under the brand name *Paysandu*, named after the town where the McCalls had the base of their successful business that was to last many decades.

Ox tongue enjoyed a reputation as a high-status food for sea voyagers in the 18th Century. The tradition developed of giving a newly-commissioned Royal Navy captain a cask of ox tongues. In the 19th century, ox tongue was considered a great luxury. It could be made soft by stewing it or it could be pickled and made hard. Breakfasts in Victorian times could be significant meals, with ox tongue being served alongside cold pies and other cooked meats.

An advert for *Paysandu* ox tongue appeared on page 12 of the edition of 26th September 1882 of *The Times from London*. In 1886, records show that McCall & Co processed 500,000 tongues in that year. On today's eBay there are many replicas of *Paysandu* wrappers dating from around 1890 offered for sale. *Paysandu* tongue was advertised in the 1892 edition of Mrs Beeton's *The Book of Household Management* containing the words *"Every Housekeeper should keep always in store a supply of McCall's **Paysandu** Ox Tongues – In Tins, from 1½ lbs to 3 lbs each – Ready for Immediate use"*. Another advertisement from the 1890's shows three people seated at a small table with the caption *"The Unexpected Guest – Bring in one of McCalls **Paysandu** Ox Tongues"*. *Paysandu Ox Tongue* was marketed in many parts of the world, including in the St John's Newfoundland where the local newspaper *The Evening Telegram* of 29th December 1904 included an advert by Ellis & Co of 203 Water Street suggesting it for *"a Reception on New Year's Day, 1905"*.

Canned ox tongue was particularly popular with polar expeditions and a tin of *Paysandu* discovered many years later at Scott's camp in the Antarctic was still found to be edible. Then, McCalls *Paysandu* tongue became part of the rations for British soldiers first in the Boer War and later in World War I. Soldiers couldn't go to war without it.

Even the novelist Sir Henry Rider Haggard wrote about McCalls' canned tongue. In Chapter 5 of his book *She,* published in 1886, he describes how his heroes landed on the shores of Africa with only preserved goods to see them through. He writes: *"Then, taking shelter from the sun under some trees, we made a hearty breakfast off a **Paysandu** potted tongue, of which we had brought a good quantity with us, congratulating ourselves loudly on our good fortune in having loaded and provisioned the boat on the previous day before the hurricane destroyed the dhow"*. He continues: *"So we lighted a lantern, and made our evening meal off another potted tongue in the best fashion that we could"*.

Still further, in *Diary of a Nobody* written by George and Weedon Grossmith (1892), there is a passage as follows: *"When Carrie prepares a little extemporised supper for friends she serves the leftovers of a cold joint, a small piece of salmon (which her husband agrees to forego lest there is insufficient to go round), blancmange, custard and jam puffs. To celebrate Lupin's engagement she makes little cakes, jam puffs (again) and jelly. Sandwiches, cold chicken, ham and some sweets also are provided. On the sideboard, for the more hungry ones to peg into if they liked', are a 'nice piece of cold beef and a* **Paysandu** *tongue."*

From 1888 William McCall spent much time in South America, with his brother Allan (see below), developing and managing the business. These were the successful years, culminating in increased demand when the Boer War started, despite a hiccup in 1898, of which more below. The business thrived and the McCalls hit another patch of good fortune and flowing profits.

In Kelly's *Merchants and Manufacturers of the World,* 1903, under Concordia, Argentina, *"McCall & Cia (tongue preserving) - Beef Preserves"* is documented as one of the family's businesses. Interestingly, this was run by George Ritchie, the grandson of Samuel Ritchie, who was William's grandfather's erstwhile business partner.

William took over as Chairman of McCall & Co when his father, John, died in 1905 and he was also appointed a Trade Arbitrator by the Preserved Food Trades' Section of the LCCI. But, increasingly, as his charitable interests took over, he left more of the running of the business to his brother, Allan, who eventually succeeded him as Chairman of the company. He was also Chairman of the Steel Barrel Co Ltd and a director of Glico Petroleum Limited.

William McCall was a devout Christian who had a sincere interest in the plight of young homeless children. Perhaps inspired by his father's Evangelical zeal, as a teenager William began working with Thomas (later Dr) Barnardo at a ragged school, in Ernest Street, off Mile End Road, where Barnardo was the Superintendent.

Ragged schools were charitable organisations dedicated to the free education of destitute children in 19th century Britain. The schools were established in working-class districts of the rapidly expanding industrial towns, beginning in the 1830's. Lord Shaftesbury was a great promoter of ragged schools and William's father would have been very familiar with the movement as a committed Evangelist who knew Shaftesbury.

Barnardo had travelled from Dublin to London in 1866 to train as a doctor at the London Hospital in Whitechapel, with the aim of becoming a missionary in China. Before commencing his medical training he took the job of Superintendent of the Ernest Street School. A few months later there was an outbreak of cholera in the East End. More than 4,000 people died in London, including 3,000 in the East End alone. This left many children homeless. Hundreds, if not thousands, of children were forced to beg and to sleep rough on the streets. Barnardo abandoned his plans to go to China. He resigned his position at the Ernest Street School in 1868 and founded the East End Juvenile Mission in Stepney, where children could get a basic education. Then, in 1870 he opened his first home for boys in Stepney Causeway where they could be trained in carpentry, metal work and shoe making. This made it more likely that they could secure an apprenticeship and gain paid work. Barnardo regularly went out at night into the slum districts to find destitute boys. After he had gathered two or three and persuaded them of the benefits of life in his home he took them back to Stepney Causeway where they were given food, clothing and some work training.

Initially Barnardo limited the number of boys who could stay at the shelter. However, a life changing moment occurred, which was witnessed by William McCall, and this story has been passed down the generations and become McCall family legend. One evening, an 11-year old homeless boy, John Somers (nicknamed "*Carrots*") was turned away because the shelter was full. Two days later he was found dead due to malnutrition and exposure, having slept the night in a sugar barrel. After this heart wrenching experience, Barnardo vowed never to turn another child away and a sign was hung up outside the shelter stating "*No Destitute Child Ever Refused Admission*".

This incident greatly affected William and he became a good friend, as well as an admirer and supporter, of Dr Barnardo. Over the years the McCall family business commitments prevented greater involvement by William in the UK based charity especially as he spent just over 10 years, from 1888 to 1899 in South America. However, on William's return to London, Dr Barnardo invited him to join the Council of Barnardo's Homes and William was present when Her Majesty Queen Victoria visited the Girls' Village Home at Barkingside.

By the time of the Doctor's death in 1905, the charity had no fewer than 96 homes, caring for more than 8,500 children. In that year, William was appointed Vice-Chairman. Then from 1920 to his death in 1929, William took on the role of Chairman of the Council of Dr Barnardo's Homes.

William McCall's funeral took place at St Peter's-in-the-Forest in Epping Forest, Walthamstow on 25 April 1929 following his death in Folkestone on the 20th. Mourners included Mrs Barnardo, members of the Council and the heads of departments of the Barnardo homes at Stepney, the Girls' Village Home, the Boys' Garden City and Goldings, north of Hertford. A memorial service was held at Barnardo's headquarters at the same time.

AE Williams, Dr Barnardo's Private Secretary and Biographer, wrote the following tribute to McCall: "*It is difficult to write of our late Chairman because he ever maintained such a consistently high level of Christian conduct. He was, indeed a loveable man, always courteous and considerate, always ready to see and give full weight to the other point of view; but when, after reviewing the evidence, and weighing the facts, his mind was made up., he took a firm stand and could not be moved.*"

In his tribute Williams also repeated a quote from *The Record* newspaper: "*The death of William McCall removed from London life one of the noblest and most self-denying figures in our philanthropic and religious world. Mr McCall lived for others; he did good because he could do nothing else, and he avoided with a modesty that is as rare as it is Christian, the publicity which others consider th reward of their good deeds. He devoted his powerful brain, shrewd insight and boundless energy to the work of God... Above everything else, he was a Christian gentleman – kind, courteous, prayerful, and ever anxious to do his master's will.*"

William McCall had four daughters. One was killed in a riding accident while a girl. William forbade the other three to marry while of childbearing age as there had been madness in his wife's family and he was afraid that it might be perpetuated. One daughter, Winifred Marion, defied him and married a Reverend Wilson, the vicar of St James Holloway, and had six children, one of whom, Basil Wilson, later joined McCall & Co. Helen Agnes died an old maid and Eva Marguerite married her beau in middle age. It is also reported that William McCall's philanthropic ideals left his three surviving daughters in financial straits at his death.

Hardy Bertram McCall (1859 - 1934)

The third of John McCall's sons was Hardy Bertram McCall. He was married twice, first in 1882 to Vida Mary Anderson, who died in 1894, and then to Maud Eleanor Macnally. By his first wife, he had two children, Thomas Hardy McCall, a Major who was killed on active service with the British Expeditionary Force in France in 1940, and Vida Mary. He had a younger son, Bertram, known as Brian.

Bertram McCall's passion was research and writing and his publications include:
- *Memoirs of My Ancestors – A Collection of Genealogical Memoranda Respecting Several Old Scottish Families*, 1884
- *Some Old Families – A Contribution to the Genealogical History of Scotland*, 1889
- *The History and Antiquities of the Parish of Mid-Calder, with some Account of the Religious House of Torphichen*, 1894
- *The early history of Bedale in the North riding of Yorkshire*, 1907
- *The Parish Registers of Kirklington in the County of York (1568-1812)*, 1909
- *Richmondshire Churches*, 1910
- Articles in the *Yorkshire Archaeological Journal*, 1912, 1923 and 1930

As a result of the detailed information included in the first two books listed above, Bertram made an enormous contribution to the research and documentation of the ancestral history of the McCall family. It is entirely due to him that we know so much about the family from the 17th century until the end of the 19th century. He was a Fellow of the Society of Antiquarians of Scotland and a member of the Council of the Yorkshire Archaeological Society and Editor of Yorkshire Archaeological Journal.

In his early career, he was also clerk to John McCall & Co in Houndsditch, as this extract from testimony given and recorded at the Central Criminal Court, better known as the Old Bailey, shows, when he gave evidence at a trial in August 1879.

Two men, Henry Goswell and John Warner were accused of unlawfully endeavouring to obtain goods by false pretences. As a witness, Bertram McCall gave the following evidence: "*I am clerk to J. McCall and Co., provision merchants of Houndsditch - on 19th June Warner came with this letter: "Gentlemen, please forward us per bearer your price list of Wilson's beef," and in the afternoon he called again with another letter on one of the same forms, which if lost, and I gave him an invoice and wrote at the bottom, "If you will hand us a cheque we will issue delivery order," and next day he brought a letter and this cheque. (This was dated 20th June, 1879, on the London and Provincial Bank for £19. 18s. 4d., signed James Harrison.) I gave him the delivery order believing the cheque to be good, but it was returned through our bankers*". Both Goswell and Warner were found guilty and each sentenced to two years' imprisonment.

Allan McCall and Family

Geographical Diversion to Tasmania

Allan McCall (1861 – 1935)

Meanwhile, Allan McCall (known as "*Tatto*"), John's fourth son, was earmarked to manage a diversification of the McCall business to Australia. In parallel with the South American venture, John McCall had plans to establish a factory in Tasmania canning rabbit and perhaps kangaroo as well as tinning fruit and making jam in the summer. This would help satisfy the growing demand by the growing population of Great Britain for canned products.

Allan was originally sent to Uruguay to study the family business. While in Uruguay he met and fell in love with an English girl, Juanita Gillespie. The match was, however, considered unsuitable and Allan was sent by his father to Australia on a business pretext.

With his father, Allan visited Hobart in about 1881 and remained there until 1886 developing and managing a new canning business. There he married, in February 1883, Ruth Helen Shoobridge (1860-1947), the youngest daughter (the thirteenth out of fourteen children) of Richard Shoobridge (1818-1891) of Glenorchy by his second marriage, to Mary Wood, his first wife having died soon after giving birth to a daughter. Mary's parents hailed from Berwick on Tweed.

In January 1788 the first British fleet of convicts arrived in Australia and Captain Arthur Philip established a penal colony at Sydney Cove with 751 convicts and 252 marines and their families. Over the next few decades more settlements were established and in the period 1803 to 1853 around 75,000 convicts were transported to Van Diemen's Land, whose name was changed to Tasmania in 1856. After a short while, it became clear that the convicts knew nothing about farming and it was difficult to make the penal colonies self-sufficient. Efforts were made to encourage *gentleman farmers* to emigrate to Australia, with mixed success. Then, the Colonial Office introduced incentives such that settlers were promised "*a grant of land upon your arrival in proportion to the means you may possess of bringing the same into cultivation.*" Discouraged by the state of the economy in England, many families risked the long voyage and the harsh conditions on arrival in Australia to forge a new life on the subcontinent.

Richard Shoobridge's father, William (1781-1836), was one of these intrepid pioneers. William and his father, also Richard, had been tenant farmers, growing hops, in Kent. Always at the mercy of the vagaries of absentee landlords, they moved from a farm in Tenterden to another near Maidstone and then to Eltham. But William had other ideas. A devout Methodist, he had faith and implicit trust in God's will and this was a source of strength in facing the hardships that were to follow.

So, in 1821, together with his pregnant wife, Mary, and their eight children, William Shoobridge left Kent on the sailing vessel *Denmark Hill*, paying £250 for steerage accommodation. Their destination was Van Diemen's Land. Steerage passengers were obliged to bring their own *Dry Provisions* while the Captain provided "*a weekly ration of salted meat, biscuit, water, fuel and candles*". The ship was due to leave on 21 November 1821 but storms prevented this; they were tied up in dock for six weeks and exhausted a good part of their rations. Their quarters, down in the hold, were cramped and, for the first part of the journey in the Northern Hemisphere, they must have been cold and damp. As they reached the Tropics and temperatures rose, conditions must have become increasingly smelly. En route, off the west coast of Africa, they lost a son and then a daughter from illness. In March, as they rounded the Cape of Good Hope, Mary gave birth to a daughter who soon died. Then, weakened by illness, sea sickness and starvation, Mary herself succumbed, as they were passing the Roaring Forties. She was buried at sea.

William Shoobridge arrived in Hobart Town on 18 May 1822 with his motherless family, including young Richard, aged four. He had goods and cash totalling £798. Lieutenant-Governor William Sorell offered him the post of superintendent of the timber yard, and he was granted twenty acres of land at Providence Valley, where he built Kent Cottage in 1823. There in 1824 he was shot at by a convict, John Logan. A metal rule in his pocket saved him from serious injury while Logan was executed in 1825 for attempted murder. Shoobridge resigned his post at the timber yard after a few years to devote himself to the production of hops at Providence Valley from sets he had brought from Kent. In this he had some success, the first marketable crop being produced in 1825 and then 453 lbs weight in 1826, 362 lbs in 1827 and 1,043 lbs in 1828; all was sold locally. In 1827 he was placed in charge of a nearby government lime kiln at a salary of £40 a year. He held this position until 1830.

William Shoobridge also acquired a farm of 700 acres in the Drummond district, now Tea Tree, and was half-owner of a mill at Battery Point. His fortunes fluctuated as the price of hops rose and then fell, but with help from colleagues and friends he remained solvent. In 1823 he was on the Wesleyan Methodist Schools' Committee for Hobart and assisted with the Methodist Mission. Later, after marrying again, his new wife being a Quaker, he attended meetings of the Society of Friends and became a lay preacher. He gave the society half an acre of Providence Valley as a burial ground and was the first person to be buried there when he died in 1836.

The early years in Van Diemen's Land were tough for William but, in Providence Valley, he established a business that was to give his children and grandchildren a reasonable level of comfort and financial stability. When William died in 1836, his son, the 18 year old Richard, took over the productive hop fields, quarry and lime kilns.

Richard Shoobridge was energetic, very hands on and a thoughtful and caring employer. As the years went by, he left the farm and orchard in Providence Valley in charge of his son, George, and moved to Glenorchy, acquiring an attractive stone built house, *Clydesdale,* where the remainder of his seven children (a further seven died in infancy) lived in some comfort. A big man, with robust build and white hair, Richard had a jovial personality and was known as the local squire.

His youngest daughter, Ruth, grew up in reasonably wealthy surroundings with a hectic social life of riding, parties and balls at Government House - a far cry from the horrors of her grandparents' voyage from Great Britain in 1821/22 and the hardships of her grandfather's early days in the colony. Stories about Ruth which have been passed down the family indicate that she was flirtatious and, with her sister, Hannah, the toast of Hobart. Clearly she was a good match for the handsome Scot, Allan McCall, a man of private means who had newly arrived in Hobart to head up the family's canning business in Tasmania.

By the 1880's there were millions of rabbits in Tasmania. Introduced to the continent in the first half of the 19th century originally for sport, they had bred rapidly; each pair could breed 40 young every year. They had become a serious threat to the land and to farming. Rabbiters became wealthy from the bounties paid for the rabbits they killed and businessmen started to make money out of canning rabbit meat. Many articles appeared in Victorian newspapers in Australia about "the rabbit problem" and about the opportunities for commercial gain.

The Hobart *Mercury* of Monday 9 January 1882 records the beginning of the McCall enterprise in Tasmania as follows: "*Our readers will remember that during last session of Parliament, correspondence was laid on the table of the House by the then Colonial Treasurer, Mr WR Giblin, in relation to the establishment of factories in Tasmania for tinning rabbits for export by the firm of Alan (sic) McCall and Co., of 137, Houndsditch, London. The firm in question asked for the exclusive right and privilege to export all tinned rabbits and hares from the colony for a period of 30 years, and also for a Government bounty of 1d (old pence) per rabbit on all exported, as well as the admission of the necessary machinery into the colony free of duty, and other minor concessions. The Government considered the number of years named for the monopoly and the amount of the bounty asked too great, but were not unwilling to grant the concessions asked, subject to modification in these respects, reducing the number of years over which the monopoly should extend to 10 years, and the bounty to £2 per ton for every ton exported. However, when the matter came before Parliament it fell through and no arrangement was come to with the firm. In the meantime the machinery had been shipped, and preparations for starting the industry made. The failure of the attempt to come to an arrangement with the Government relative to the establishment of factories on the proposed basis did not discourage the enterprising promoters, and they have determined, notwithstanding the rebuff they met with, to establish a factory in our midst. A company has been floated in London bearing the title of The Tasmanian Preserving and Trading Co., with a nominal capital of £50,000,* [approximately £5 million in today's money] *all the shares in which have been taken up. Mr John McCall, the senior member of the Landon firm of McCall and Co., accompanied by his son, Mr. Alan (sic) McCall, arrived in this colony some time back, and has since been engaged in looking for a suitable site on which to establish the factory. After some considerable trouble it was determined to secure a portion of land near the Rosetta Crossing, on the Main Line of Railway, and in Glenorchy. Negotiations were opened with Mr Wm. Overell, and 9 acres of land were purchased from that gentleman, with a frontage on the main road. To secure a frontage on the river, 3 acres of this land was exchanged for a similar amount belonging to Mr Wm. Hallam on the bank of the Derwent, and by these means a good property having access to river, railway line, and main road was secured. It is proposed to build on this land nearly square block of buildings about 170 yards long and 150 yards wide, in which extensive and powerful machinery will be placed. A jetty will then be run out into the stream, where schooners or steam launches can be conveniently loaded for transport to outward-bound vessels, as the trade will be almost exclusively with the home country. The business of the company will be directed to tinning game, principally rabbits, and also wild duck, kangaroo, etc., in the winter time, when the cold weather will be in favour of this branch of preserving. In summer time fruit preservation will be the principal business of the firm. By fruit preserving is not merely meant the making of jam, but the tinning of raspberries, strawberries, cherries, etc, in a whole state, after the American manner, a fashion in which our large-sized and well-*

flavoured fruits would no doubt sell in the English and Continental markets to great advantage. At first about 50 workpeople will be employed in the factory, but as the trade is opened up, the magnitude of the business will no doubt increase, and the number of hands employed be larger. By the careful management of resources, it is believed that the factory can be kept open throughout the whole year. The firm of Messrs. McCall, of which the gentleman now in Hobart is the senior member, have no less than five preserving factories in South America, so that if business experience and thorough knowledge of the details of preserving on a large scale can make the venture successful, it could not be better favoured in this respect than it is Mr Alan (sic) McCall will be the manager of the Tasmanian company".

Some eight months later the Hobart *Mercury* of Wednesday 2 August 1882 updated their news as follows: "*In January last it was announced in these columns that a company had been formed in London, bearing the title of The Tasmanian Preserving and Trading Co. On behalf of the company, Mr John McCall, the senior member of the London firm of McCall and Co (which has no less than five preserving factories in South America), came out to this colony, accompanied by his son, Mr Alan (sic) McCall, and secured land at Glenorchy a site for a factory. Preserving operations have been carried on to a certain extent for some weeks past, a staff of about 30 workpeople being employed. Owing to the many difficulties that always are in any new enterprise, the manager has not been able to preserve the number of rabbits he would have liked, but he trusts next season to be able to put up, from 15,000 to 18,000 weekly. The rabbits are brought by mail train to O'Brien's Bridge from the various depots opened on the Main Line for the receipt of game, and thence are carted. They come to hand four mornings in the week, Saturday being excepted, owing to no preservation, of course, being done on the Sunday, and Monday being excepted for the very sufficient reason that no mail train arrives that morning. Some particulars of the modus operandi of rabbit preservation, as adopted in the establishment, may prove of interest. The rabbits are received in the kitchen. Here they are hung on hooks, and undergo the first operation- skinning, As soon as skinned the rabbit is cast on to a block, and is deftly relieved of the unnecessary appendages of head and feet. The little carcass is next passed on to a table, whereon it is cleaned and wiped with a cloth. It is than cut up into joints, which, after being washed in a tank of cold water, are placed in brine till next morning. When this comes round, the rabbit meat is washed in warm water, and packed in tins. All the joints of one rabbit are put in one tin, the weight of the contents of which is then made up to 2 1bs net. The top of the tin is put in, and this finishes the process gone through in the kitchen. The filled tin is taken into the Soldering-up shop, and soldered up, a small vent-hole being, however, left in the top of the tin, for the escape of air. The Preserving-room has next to be entered. Here there are a number of preserving baths, each of which is made to contain about 250 tins. The Soldered-up tin is put into a bath, and left to steam till all the air is driven out of the tin through the vent-hole. About two hours usually suffices and this done, the tin is subjected to a high pressure to test the Soldering. The tins are then brought into the printing and lacquering room. The tins are here polished, after which the name, brand, etc., of the company is printed on them, by rolling them one by one over an India rubber stamp. The brand, of course, is a Bunny and the letter print sets forth that he, as preserved by the Tasmanian Preserving and Trading Co. (Limited), of which Alex (sic) McCall is manager, and for which John McCall and Co,, London are sole agents and is "for curry and fricassee, for ragout and rabbit-pie, and delectable cither hot or cold*".

The *Launceston Examiner* of 3 April 1884 reported that the Tasmanian Preserving and Trading Company, Hobart, had been awarded a second class certificate and bronze medal for its preserved rabbits in *The Calcutta Exhibition* of 1884.

During the period 1883 to 1885, the Hobart *Mercury* reported the exports of rabbits and jam by the Tasmanian Preserving and Trading Co Limited as follows:
- On 19 February 1883, via the *Tasman* for Sydney: 250 cases of jam
- On 16 July 1883, via the *Southern Cross* bound for Melbourne: 200 cases of preserved rabbits, eight bales of rabbit skins and one case of jam
- On 8 August 1883, via the barque *Loongana* bound for Auckland: 50 cases of jam
- On 8 October 1883, via the *Tasman* bound for Sydney: 50 cases of jam
- On 21 July 1884, via the *Southern Cross* bound for Melbourne: 250 cases of preserved rabbits
- On 5 January 1885, via the *Flora* bound for Sydney: 11 cases of preserved rabbits

Then in the edition of 18 December 1885 of the *Launceston Examiner*, an advert appeared as follows: "*Tasmanian Preserving and Trading Company, Limited – Tenders are invited and will be received up to December 30th for the purchase of the above Company's rabbit and fruit preserving factory and plant at Glenorchy, Tasmania. Tenders to be addressed to the manager of the Company, Glenorchy, Tasmania, from whom all particulars and information can be obtained – Allan McCall*".

In those days the cargoes of most ships were recorded in local newspapers together with ships' sailings. While it is possible that there were other exports of cans of preserved rabbits and jam by the Tasmanian Preserving and Trading Company, the above shipments do not suggest a thriving business which would have covered the costs and provided a return on the capital outlay. The advert seeking tenders in December 1885 was also an ominous sign that not all was well financially. On top of this, there is a story that was passed down orally through the family that the Tasmanian venture had not been a commercial success. £50,000 (or about £5 million in today's money) had been invested in the venture and it is possible that much if not most of this was lost.

The consolation, if there was one, was that Allan had found a wife, Ruth Shoobridge, and was about to have a family. He was not yet 27 but one imagines that he must have learnt a great deal.

Allan and Ruth were married in St Paul's Church, Glenorchy, Tasmania in February 1883 and their two elder children, Allan Bertram and William George (known as "Mac") were born in Glenorchy and nearby Ivadene. Young Allan Bertram died within a few days of his birth but Mac survived and his story is told in a further chapter below.

It may have taken Allan (senior) some time to sell or close down the business, after which he and Ruth moved to Sydney for a few years. They rented a house, *Rosendahl*, a spacious bungalow in Mosman Bay, an attractive area north of Sydney Harbour.

Children of Allan McCall & Ruth Shoobridge

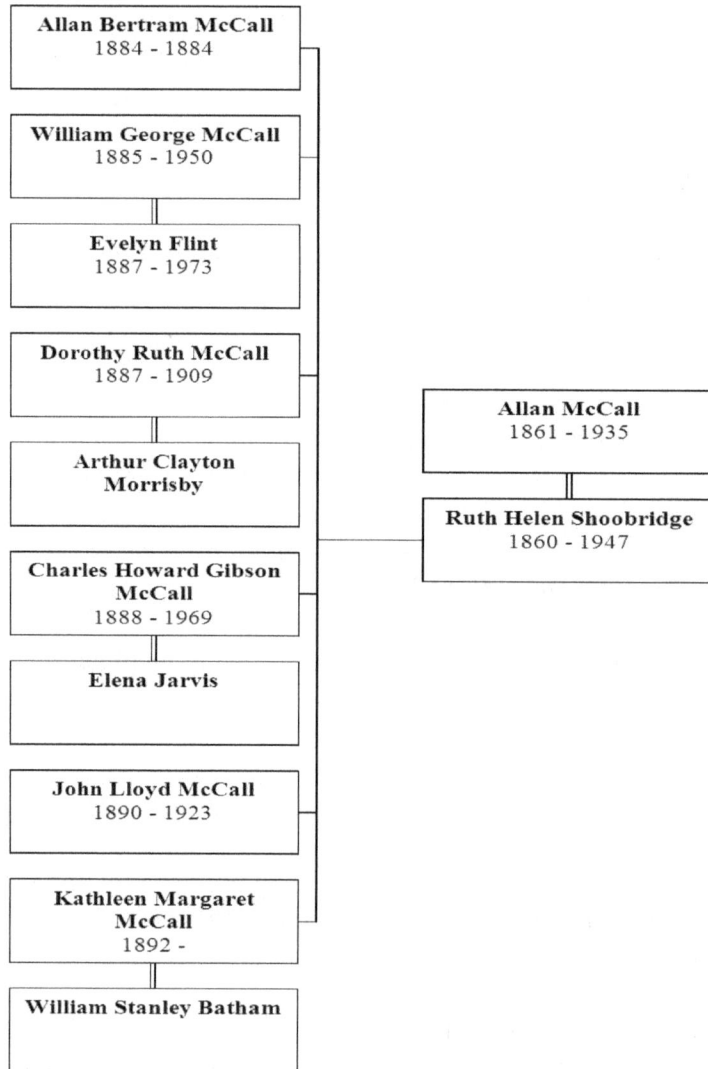

Allan Bertram McCall 1884 - 1884	
William George McCall 1885 - 1950	
Evelyn Flint 1887 - 1973	
Dorothy Ruth McCall 1887 - 1909	Allan McCall 1861 - 1935
Arthur Clayton Morrisby	Ruth Helen Shoobridge 1860 - 1947
Charles Howard Gibson McCall 1888 - 1969	
Elena Jarvis	
John Lloyd McCall 1890 - 1923	
Kathleen Margaret McCall 1892 -	
William Stanley Batham	

Allan and Ruth had the following children who survived their childhood:

- William George McCall (known as "Mac"), born 24 August 1885 in Hobart, Tasmania
- Dorothy Ruth McCall, born 2 March 1887 in Sydney, New South Wales, Australia. She married (Arthur) Clayton Morrisby in 1907 and emigrated to Southern Rhodesia, where she died from typhoid fever on 15 May 1909 in the town of Hartley
- Charles Howard Gibson McCall, (see below), born 27 September 1888 in Sydney, New South Wales, Australia and died in 1969 in Buenos Aires, Argentina
- John Lloyd McCall (known as "Jack"), born 16 August 1890 in Walthamstow, England and died on 3 December 1923 in Sutton, Surrey, England
- Kathleen Margaret McCall (known as "Katie"), born 9 June 1892 in Walthamstow, England. She married William Stanley Batham in September 1914

During their time in Australia, one imagines that Allan's job was acting as agent, liaising with the Australian companies who were using McCalls' patented technology to can produce for export and then distribution through McCall & Co in Houndsditch, London.

By 1888, Allan and Ruth had moved to the UK, where they acquired a house, *Horndon*, in Walthamstow. This was close to *Woodlands*, the home that his eldest brother, William (1851-1929), had inherited from his father, John McCall, in 1879 and where William lived with his wife and four daughters. Walthamstow, close to Epping Forest, was, in those days, a fashionable suburb of London and they lived in considerable style.

Family stories have it that when Allan took his new wife to Scotland to present her to some members of his family, his ugly, sour faced aunts dismissed the bride as "*a wee pairson of nae presence.*" They are reputed to have been a very narrow straight laced lot. Certainly their description of Ruth does not at all accord with that ascribed to her when a young woman back in Hobart. Ruth loved her father-in-law, John, nicknamed *The Ron*, but found all her other new relatives cold and unkind.

For the next 10 years, from 1888 to 1898, Allan worked intermittently in London and South America, helping his elder brother, William, develop further and manage their ox tongue canning business. The Census Return of 1891 shows Allan, Ruth and their children residing in Walthamstow.

McCall & Co were at that stage paying 90% dividends on the shares, all of which were owned by the family as it was not a public company.

Cycling was beginning to become fashionable among the middle classes of Great Britain and Allan belonged to the Cyclists' Touring Club; he and Ruth would tour on a tandem. The business more or less ran itself and life must have been very agreeable.

Then the children contracted chickenpox. Ruth caught it very badly and was declared an invalid. They all moved to Falmouth, with its balmy climate, in Cornwall, where they lived from 1895 to 1898. They rented *Penmere Manor*, an attractive house (now a hotel) at Penryn. They had a carriage and horses, two yachts, the *Fairlight* and the *Tattywag*, together with a large staff of servants, nurses and governesses. London and the business world seemed very far away.

Dorothy, Katie, Charlie, Jack, Mac. Penmere, Falmouth, 1895–1898

Allan McCall's children at Penmere Manor, Falmouth, Cornwall

The Rollercoaster Years

The period 1888 to 1898 were golden years for McCall & Co. The South American business had developed well. Canned tongue had become a favourite in Victorian households. *Paysandu* was a well-known brand name. Sales were booming. The company was flourishing. There was not a cloud in the sky.

But, towards the end of the 19th century, things started to go wrong for McCall & Co. Major concerns were being expressed about the meatpacking industry. This had undoubtedly prompted John McCall (1824-1905) to take such a prominent role as Chairman of the Preserved Food Trades' Section of the London Chamber of Commerce & Industry between 1884 and 1903. In his early years in business he had witnessed the Goldner scandal and now he did all he could to encourage best practice in the industry regarding standards of safety and hygiene.

In 1898 the Press in the United States reported that a major Chicago company, Armour & Co, had supplied tons of rotten canned beef to the US Army in Cuba during the Spanish-American War. The meat had been packed in tins along with a visible layer of boric acid, which was thought to act as a preservative, and was used to mask the stench of the rotten meat. Troops fell ill and were unfit for combat; some died. This affected the reputation of all meat canners, including McCall & Co.

The US scandal and its impact on the family business may well have prompted Allan McCall to return from Cornwall for, in 1898, he, Ruth and their children moved back to the south east. They lived at *The Chestnuts,* (a house in Egham, Surrey where Lewis Carroll often stayed while visiting his sisters and which Ruth described as "*a horrid little house*"). Some years later her daughter, Kathleen (known as "*Katie*"), went in search of her childhood home and found a very substantial house with a large garden. So, it appears, poverty was relative.

Allan increasingly took over responsibility from his brother William for management of the company which was then based at 6, Eastcheap EC1, near the Monument in the City. He assumed the role of Managing Director. For a short time the business struggled but, with the advent of the Boer War (1899 to 1902), demand by soldiers for canned meat saw the company's performance improve. Dividends to the family increased and, as a consequence, in 1901, the family moved to a more spacious dwelling, *Wedmore*, at Henley on Thames.

Everything suddenly seemed to be going well. However, there was another major upset, caused by the publication in 1906 of a novel, *The Jungle*, written by Upton Sinclair, about meat canning in Chicago, where hygiene and human safety were low priorities. Stories were related about the big powered meat choppers slicing off men's hands and fingers which then fell into the rest of the meat and were duly part of the canned or frozen meat product. The worst part was the suggestion that a man fell into the meat grinders while production continued. The book caused a major stir. Sales of canned meats stopped abruptly. For very many months McCalls had to hold huge stocks since, if production ceased, the tongues from the *saladeros* on the River Plate would have been diverted to the new refrigerating plants. Things were tough for a number of years. The company's results suffered.

But, public perception changed again. The meat canning business recovered and, with it, the McCall family fortunes. Allan and Ruth moved to Bedenwell, a big country house at Belvedere in the Borough of Bexley in Kent and finally to Sevenoaks.

In 1913, a book, *Twentieth Century Impressions of Brazil*, described Bage in the state of Rio Grande do Sol in Southern Brazil. There is reference to McCall & Co's Paysandu enjoying "*the best reputation worldwide*". At that time the company had four factories in Brazil: Bage, Pelotas, Sant'Anna and Quaraim; three in Uruguay: El Cerro, Paysandu and Rio Negro; two in Argentina in Concordia and Gualeguaychu. The book recorded that 100,000 tongues were exported each year from Bage alone, mostly to England.

World War I brought an enormous increase in demand by soldiers for canned meat. The sales of tongue took off. As noted earlier, in 1886 McCall's total exports from South America were 500,000 tongues a year; so at the peak, with nine factories, the total production might have reached almost 1 million, which amounts in today's money to a revenue of around £5 million or as much as £10 million at retail prices.

In his role as Managing Director and then Chairman, Allan continued to visit South America before and after the First World War, as shown by ships' passenger lists of departures:
- Date of outward passage not known
- 13 May 1913 - Buenos Aires to Southampton
- 18 February 1921 - Southampton to Pernambuco, Brazil
- 6 June 1921 - River Plate, South America to Southampton
- 29 May 1925 - Southampton to Montevideo, Uruguay (accompanied by Ruth)
- 13 July 1925 - Buenos Aires, Argentina to Southampton (accompanied by Ruth)
- 21 March 1929 - Southampton to Montevideo, Uruguay
- 4 June 1929 - Buenos Aires, Argentina to Southampton

Allan McCall continued as Chairman of McCalls until he died in 1935 in Sevenoaks, Kent, aged 73.

Like his father he was active in public life. In his spare time he was a keen sailor. He did a great deal to promote dinghy sailing and small boat racing for young people on the east coast of England. He was, at one time Commodore of the Royal Corinthian Yacht Club and a member of the Royal Thames Yacht Club. He kept his yacht, *The Kathleen*, at Felixstowe and had a launch on the Thames when they lived at Henley.

No-one knows precisely why Allan McCall was given the nickname *Tatto*. Certainly the younger generation knew him by this name. In Latin America, the name is occasionally used as a pet name and as a term of endearment for an elderly relation. Allan's grandchildren remember Tatto as being "*extraordinarily silent*" but very competent with his hands – both metal and wood working. He apparently spent many hours in his workshop. He has been described as very reserved and unable to express warmth or affection and was "*a very sad man*". Perhaps the vagaries of his business life had not given him cause for much personal satisfaction. Certainly running McCall & Co between 1898 and the 1920's must have been challenging, with a few periods of great success and then a few of great concern. After huge demand for the McCalls' products in the Boer War and the First World War, the company probably did not thrive as much during the post war years. Then, in 1923, his eldest son, Jack, his heir apparent, died. No wonder he was sad, reflecting on this and the current financial performance of the business compared to the prosperity of earlier times.

On Allan's death in 1935, his widow Ruth moved to Gerrards Cross in Buckinghamshire. There she is remembered by her granddaughter-in-law, Jean Batham (nee Jagoe), as a much loved grandmother who was still pretty, albeit a trifle stout, had great charm and was very polite to whomsoever she met. She always dressed in black and, when indulging in her favourite pastime of gardening, she wore a large hat and a voluminous black apron.

As Jean Batham wrote in her description of her husband's family, *"[Ruth] must have been a beautiful woman and there was a sort of zany quality about her that I suspect enabled her to float through life on her own little private cloud nine. She would go shopping in the village, invariably greeting the shopkeepers or bank clerks with a smiling **Good morning, Mr So and So. It's a beautiful day today**. Whether it was sunshine, sleet or snow, they would invariably reply **Yes, Mrs McCall. Good morning Mrs McCall**."*

And then, *"Spring cleaning was an annual ritual which she undertook with an ingrained sense of duty, if not of pleasure. Regular letters were written each Sunday to her large and scattered family as she sat by the fire, the drawing room door always ajar and winter's icy blast airing the room. She was the kindest of employers but was serenely convinced that the working class were a different breed of human. At one time we were all discussing the introduction of a Bill regularising the introduction of holidays with pay for factory workers. **But why**, she said plaintively, **do these people need holidays? They never used to**. It was a strange and unfamiliar world that crept up around her during the war years and she was a child of her time."*

In spite of Ruth's old fashioned ideas, Jean records being *"struck by the real affection and regard that everyone, family and friends had for her."*

Ruth died at her home in Gerrards Cross in 1947, aged 87.

William George ("Mac") McCall
(1886 – 1950)

The End of the British McCall Line in Merchanting

Jack McCall (1890 – 1923)

Although not the eldest son of Allan and Ruth, Jack McCall was earmarked to head up the London end of McCall & Co's business. However, his early death at the age of 33 in 1923 meant that William McCall (known as "*Mac*") had to step in.

William George McCall (1885 – 1950)

Mac was Allan's eldest surviving son, born at Ivadene, Hobart New Town, Tasmania, in 1885. He was brought to the UK by his parents when he was two years old and the family lived in Walthamstow. He became involved in McCall & Co in his late teens and he is recorded in a ship's passenger list as travelling to South America when he was aged 19, returning from La Plata, Argentina, to London, arriving 5 June 1915. In the same year, he married Evelyn Flint (otherwise known as "*Enon*" or "*Gandi*"), the granddaughter of Henry Flint, a Mayor of Newbury.

Mac's heart was in engineering and worked for a time in Manchester for a firm that made automotive components. There, his only child, Dorothy Elizabeth, was born on 1 May 1919.

He then moved to Ludlow where he owned and managed an engineering business making precision tools. Tragically the factory burnt down and, being uninsured, he sought other employment. He was offered a job and took responsibility for managing the London end of the business of McCall & Co from his father. At that time, in the 1920's, the company's office was based at King William Street House, Arthur Street, London EC4. He later became Chairman of McCall & Co on the death of his father, Allan, in 1935.

Refrigeration was gradually becoming a more accepted and lower cost method of preserving meat for export. Argentina was the first country, being the most advanced, in South America to adopt this technology and put up frigorificos. For commercial reasons, McCall & Co were forced out. In Uruguay, the factory at Paysandu was closed down and another at El Cerro, run by George Ritchie, was shut down in about 1920. Concordia was also closed. In Brazil, business at the factory at Pelotas ceased in 1928 while the other two factories, at Bage and Tupancireta, continued until after World War II. There was competition from other canned meat suppliers such as Fray Bentos and Vestey, who had greater financial resources.

Mac has been described as lugubrious and not a very happy person. On photographs he always looks stern but then photographs of that era often show men looking stiff and formal. In his spare time, he built six model steam railway trains (5 inch gauge) as a hobby. Moving from Ludlow to London, they lived first in Denham and then in Gerrards Cross, where he had a model railway track that ran around his garden. In the summer months, the boiler would get fired up and adults as well as young children were given rides on his steam train.

Mac died in April 1950 at Gerrards Cross where his widow, Enon, continued to live until her early eighties. She moved to be closer to her daughter, Elizabeth, and her husband Geoffrey, Daish and their daughters, Judy and Lesley, near Kenilworth. Enon died in 1973, aged 85.

Charles McCall (1888-1969)

When he was aged 17, Charlie McCall was sent to Bage in Brazil, where the principal canning factory of McCalls was then situated. Charlie looked after the production side of the business while his father, Allan and then Mac and later his nephew, Basil Wilson, handled the sales and administration in London.

Charlie was a big, jovial, expansive man with a loud voice and a boisterous laugh. He had a passion for fishing, hunting and other outdoor pursuits. He married an English girl Elena Davies, who had spent her life in Brazil and was the daughter of Juanita (nee Gillespie) whom Allan had been forced to leave behind in South America when he was sent to Tasmania in 1881, aged 20. Elena was Anglo-Uruguayan, of Welsh descent, whose father worked for the Central Uruguay Railway Company and was one of the founders of the famed Penarol Football Club from Montevideo. There is a moving story, recorded by Jean Batham, of Charlie's visit to the UK shortly after marrying Elena. His parents, Allan and Ruth, were on the quayside to meet them and as the two young people lent over the side of the ship and waved to them, Allan turned white and clutched Ruth's arm, murmuring "*Juanita, it's Juanita*". Later when they went home and the first excitement of their reunion had quietened, Allan took Elena's watch and asked her to open the back and look inside. There was a tiny photograph and an inscription inside the watch "*From A. McC. To Juanita*". "Why, that's my Mother!" said Elena. It was indeed and Charlie had married his father's former girlfriend's daughter.

Allegedly, according to Jean Batham, Charlie missed a fortune by a hair's breadth. One day, Charlie and George Ritchie were walking home from the McCall factory in Buenos Aires when they came across an auction of plots of land which were situated on the outskirts of the city. Having just been paid, they decided to spend all their earnings on as much land as they could afford. Later these plots increased greatly in value as the city grew but when President Peron came to power he introduced legislation forbidding foreigners from owning land in Argentina and their land was confiscated.

Periodically, Charlie and Elena travelled to the UK and their return journey to Bage in December 1926 is recorded by a young employee, Jimmy Tait, aged 16. Charlie had recruited Jimmy, at that time out of work in the UK during the General Strike, to spend four years in Brazil as a Production Assistant. Jimmy describes their journey from Southampton to Bage with Charlie's two twin boys, Allan and Obbie, then aged four years old. During their passage to Bage, the ship stopped at Rio de Janeiro where, after hiring a car for three days while the ship unloaded and reloaded, Charlie and the family toured the neighbouring countryside and, then, Charlie bought a marmoset, a small monkey, to take back to Bage. The McCall factory and their home were in the middle of nowhere, with few creature comforts. After arriving in Montevideo, the entourage caught the train to Melo in north-eastern Uruguay, where they were met by a lorry with a Model T Ford on the back. The family drove in the car, getting stuck from time to time and being rescued by the lorry, while Jimmy travelled in the cab with the driver who was adept at avoiding the potholes and also pulling the family car out of the mud. The roads got worse; they crossed the border into Brazil; there were three rivers without bridges to negotiate; they journeyed to Bage and, then, along a very rough muddy track to the factory and their home some 7 miles beyond Bage.

According to Jimmy Tait's diary, life in Bage at that time was fairly basic. The business was going well but the creature comforts for the family were still being developed. At its peak, during the ox-tongue canning season, there were 65 employees, reducing to 15 during the fallow period. The local slaughterhouses were each capable of processing 300 carcasses a day, after which the tongues were brought to the McCall factory by horse and cart. Gradually as the business prospered, the lifestyle of the McCalls improved. New houses were built for Charlie's family, Jimmy and his colleague, fellow Englishman "Willie" Wilson. During the slack months, the factory machinery was overhauled, preparation was made for the coming canning season and the family, Jimmy and Willie went on fishing and hunting trips. Charlie had a caravan complete with broadcasting facilities with which he was able to keep in touch with events at the factory. They would take off for days at a time – fishing, shooting, cooking by campfires and enjoying an outdoor life. There were many mishaps. An outboard motor from the family's boat fell into the river, but was retrieved. Jimmy was bitten on the toe by a snake after which Charlie took his hunting knife, sliced open the toe in the area of the bite and filled it with potassium permanganate crystals, after which Jimmy recovered and survived. A terrible incident occurred when a machine was being repaired in an inspection pit and, while the petrol had been removed from the machine, there was an explosive mixture in the pit which was accidentally ignited by one of the mechanics lighting a cigarette. Both twin sons and two mechanics were badly burned, with scars for the rest of their lives. Charlie and his family were rather accident prone. A most tragic example of this occurred at the end of a pigeon shoot when one of the dogs was nosing around the dead birds. As recorded by Jimmy Tait, Charlie, shot gun in hand, tried to keep the dog from the birds. Accidentally the gun went off and his daughter, "Little" Elena, received the full force of the 12 bore in her chest, dying immediately.

But Charlie ran the business in Bage well and he loved his outdoor, expansive life and the freedom which he gained from running his own factory, very many miles away from civilisation. He was a true pioneer, who relished the challenging environment, enjoying the wild Brazilian "outback" and simple family pleasures. He was a strong man, a larger than life character, more physical than cerebral. Frequently, he had some quite zany ideas and extravagant gestures. But he contributed to the management of the family business in South America. He is much loved by those that knew him. They say he had a very warm heart and was very generous, showering presents on those he came to visit back in England.

The Latin way of bookkeeping and accounting was for many decades different from the Anglo-Saxon model where ethics and transparency were much more likely to be followed. There were often three sets of books – one for the tax man, another for the accountants and the shareholders and, finally, the real set which showed what was actually happening in the business. These real set of books showed that storm clouds were looming for the McCall tongue canning business in the Southern Hemisphere. In the meat trade, as refrigeration began to take over from saltification, the supply of tongues for canning began to dry up. Frozen foods became increasingly popular while the demand for canned goods reduced. Some of the McCall competitors, Vesteys, Fray Bentos and Borthwicks were larger and had great financial resources. But, even they felt the pressures of changing technology, the impact of World War 2 and changing political and trading ties. As noted earlier, the McCalls' South American factories in Argentina and Uruguay closed in the 1920's and 1930's, while the remaining two factories, at Bage and Tupancireta in Brazil, continued until after the Second World War.

The last generation of McCalls in McCall & Co

Charlie's twin sons, Allan Gibson McCall and Osborne Thomas McCall (known as "*Obbie*"), were earmarked to manage the South American end of the business where the family lived. Allan and Obbie were born in Montevideo and educated in Buenos Aires. They knew South America well.

Since Mac had no son, his sister Katie's son, Alan Batham, was asked to join the firm in London at the age of 17 as a potential successor of the next generation. Alan was sent to Brazil to gain some insight into the production side of the business. After marriage and after service in the Second World War in the Navy on convoy escort duty, Alan returned to McCall & Co which, by that time, had moved its head office to St James's Street, W1.

Mac died in 1950 and the two daughters of William McCall, Helen and Eva, as the largest shareholders in the business became more involved. Helen became Chairman and was, allegedly, opposed to innovation and modernisation.

In the 1950's, Helen introduced her nephew, Basil Wilson, as her potential successor as Chairman and Managing Director. According to Jean Batham, Alan's wife, this did not bode well for the company. McCall & Co did not adapt to the changes taking place in the industry. Refrigeration was becoming more accepted as a means of preserving and transporting meat. New methods of packaging were being introduced but Basil, as Chairman, was opposed to such ideas. Alan Batham left the firm in 1957 and a year later sailed to the West Indies in search of a new life. Other companies in the canning and packaging industry, such as Vestey, had greater foresight and also financial muscle. Gradually McCall & Co lost its way. It became loss-making and, in April 1964, the shareholders passed a resolution that the company should be "wound up voluntarily".

The South American end of the business continued for a further decade after being acquired by Charlie, and his son, Allan McCall. The other twin son, Obbie, advised his father that he was making a big mistake in buying the production end of the business and, after leaving the firm, he joined Vesteys.

In 1964, a typhoid outbreak in Aberdeen in Scotland was traced to Fray Bentos in Uruguay. Investigations revealed that the cooling water used in the canning process at the plant was not being consistently chlorinated. Britain's entry into the Common Market affected trade patterns. These factors together had a serious impact on sales to the UK of canned meat from South America. The Fray Bentos factory was given to the Uruguay Government in 1971.

Following Charlie's death in 1969, the McCall factories at Bage and Tupancireta also closed in 1971. The McCall preserved meats and canning business had lasted 120 years – not bad for a family business in which technology, trading regulations and tastes were changing.

Obbie retired to the UK in 1980 with his wife, Priscilla (Cilla), and their three children, Caroline, Stephen and Nick. Obbie died in 1989 and Cilla in 2015.

McCall & Co, in its different guises and locations, had come to an end - after 270 years of endeavour, success and failure.

Epitaph

For 270 years, the McCalls experienced a rollercoaster.

One moment, they enjoyed business success, prosperity and wealth; next moment they had to sell property, live frugally and look for new opportunities.

They took risks and invested – with mixed success.

They were resolute, entrepreneurial, flexible and adaptable.

They were not frightened of moving away from home; yet they retained roots and ties with family and friends.

They took advantage of the changing political and economic climate; and they were also sometimes adversely affected by these changes.

They embraced new technology; but sometimes they did not react soon enough.

They endured hardship and they also lived well.

Their environment was forever changing – like the Dumfries weather they left behind.

Bibliography

I am grateful to the following for information and for extracts repeated in this book:

- A British Meat Cannery in Moldavia (1844–52), Constantin Ardeleanu, The Slavonic and East European Review, 2012
- A Glasgow Tobacco Merchant during the American War of Independence: Alexander Speirs of Elderslie, 1775 to 1781, TM Devine, The William and Mary Quarterly, Omohundro Institute of Early American History and Culture, 1976
- A History of the Frozen Meat Grade, James Troubridge Critchell & Joseph Raymond, Constable & Company, 1912
- Australian Dictionary of Biography, JR Morris, 1967
- Australian Government website, 2015
- Australian Meat Products to the UK in the 19th Century – Technology Push and Market Pull, KTH Farrer, Sir Robert Menzies Centre for Australian Studies, University of London, 1988
- EastGlasgowHistory website, 2015
- Enumeration of the Inhabitants of the City of Glasgow, James Cleland, 1832
- Feeding Nelson's Navy: The True Story of Food at Sea in the Georgian Era, Janet Macdonald, Frontline Books, 2014
- Glasgow & the Tobacco Lords, Norman Nichol, Longmans, Green and Co Ltd, 1966
- Glasgow's East End – From Bishops to Barraboys, Nuala Naughton, Mainstream Publishing, Transworld Publishers, Random House Group, 2014
- Glasgow's tobacco lords: an examination of wealth creators in the eighteenth century, Carolyn Marie Peters (1990)
- Historic Tinned Food, Professor JC Drummond, GS Wilson, WR Lewis & T Macara, International Tin Research & Development Council, 1939
- James Tait's Memories (1926 – 1937)
- Memoirs of My Ancestors – A Collection of Genealogical Memoranda Respecting Several Old Scottish Families, Hardy Bertram McCall, 1884
- London Chamber of Commerce & Industry - Annual reports and information provided by its archivist, David Senior
- Scotcities website, Gerald Blaikie, 2015
- Scottish Phrase and Fable, Ian Crofton, Birlinn Limited, 2012
- Some Old Families – A Contribution to the Genealogical History of Scotland, HB McCall, FSA, 1889
- Taste, Trade and Technology – The Development of the International Meat Industry since 1840, Richard Perren, Ashgate Publishing Limited, 2006
- Technology in Australia, Australian Science and Technology Heritage Centre, 2000
- The Agrarian History of England and Wales, Joan Thirsk and EJT Collins, Cambridge University Press, 2000
- The Atlantic Economy during the 17th and 18th Centuries, edited by Peter A Coclanis, University of South Carolina Press, 2005
- Correspondence of Archibald McCall and George McCall, 1777-1783, edited by Joseph S Ewing, The Virginia Magazine of History and Biography, Vol. 73, No. 3 (Jul., 1965), pp. 312-353, The Virginia Historical Society
- The Development of Transportation in Modern England, WT Jackman, Cambridge University Press, 1916
- TheGlasgowStory website, 2015
- The Historical Society of Pennsylvania, Collection 1786, McCall family Papers, 1764-1891
- The Jungle, Upton Sinclair, Doubleday, Jabber & Company, 1906
- The McCalls, Francis Lockhart McCall, 1993
- The Social Life of Scotland in the Eighteenth Century, H Grey Graham, 1899
- The story of how the tin can nearly wasn't, Tom Geoghegan, BBC News Magazine, 2013
- Twentieth Century Impressions of Brazil: Its History, People, Commerce, Industries, and Resources, W Feldwick, LT Delaney, Arnold Wright, Lloyd's Greater Britain Publishing Company Limited, 1913
- Virginia Ghosts, Mrs Marguerite du Pont Lee, Clearfield, 1993
- You must never forget, dear children – you have ancestors, Jean Batham, 1981

www.ingramcontent.com/pod-product-compliance
Lightning Source LLC
Chambersburg PA
CBHW081156090426

42736CB00017B/3354